Shopping As an Entertainment Experience

Shopping As an Entertainment Experience

Mark Moss

LEXINGTON BOOKS

A division of
ROWMAN & LITTLEFIELD PUBLISHERS, INC.
Lanham • Boulder • New York • Toronto • Plymouth, UK

LEXINGTON BOOKS

A division of Rowman & Littlefield Publishers, Inc.
A wholly owned subsidiary of The Rowman & Littlefield Publishing Group, Inc.
4501 Forbes Boulevard, Suite 200
Lanham, MD 20706

Estover Road
Plymouth PL6 7PY
United Kingdom

British Library Cataloguing in Publication Information Available

Library of Congress Cataloging-in-Publication Data

Moss, Mark Howard, 1962–
  Shopping as an entertainment experience / Mark Moss.
    p. cm.
  ISBN-13: 978-0-7391-1681-4 (pbk. : alk. paper)
  ISBN-10: 0-7391-1681-9 (pbk. : alk. paper)
  ISBN-13: 978-0-7391-1680-7 (cloth : alk. paper)
  ISBN-10: 0-7391-1680-0 (cloth : alk. paper)
  1. Department stores—Social aspects. 2. Shopping malls—Social aspects. 3.
Shopping—Social aspects. I. Title
  HF5461.M67 2007
  306.3'4—dc22   2006038197

Printed in the United States of America

∞™ The paper used in this publication meets the minimum requirements of
American National Standard for Information Sciences—Permanence of Paper for
Printed Library Materials, ANSI/NISO Z39.48–1992.

This book is dedicated to
Merilyn and Marvin, Elly, and Steve.

Contents

Acknowledgments

I wish to thank Maria Vasilodimitrakis for all her help and suggestions. She took the time to read numerous drafts and her advice was much appreciated. Acknowledgments as well to my mother, Phyllis, and the following colleagues: Dave Phillips and Peter Meehan.

Parts of this work first appeared in the *Popular Culture Review* XIV, no. 2 (2003) and XV, no. 1 (2004).

Versions of this work were also presented at the following conferences:

"Shopping as an Entertainment Experience." Presented at the Mid-Atlantic Popular Culture/American Culture Association Conference, Silver Spring, Maryland (November 2–4, 2001).

"Dressing History: Nostalgia and Class in the Worlds of Ralph Lauren." Presented at the 32nd Annual Popular Culture Association Conference, Toronto, Canada (March 2002).

"Museum Gift Stores: Culture and Commerce." Presented at New Perspectives on Popular Culture, Technology and Society II, Seneca College (June 24, 2004).

"Liminality, Space, and the Pleasure of the Shopping Place." Presented at New Perspectives on Popular Culture, Technology and Society III, Seneca College (June 28, 2005).

Preface

Many people are split over the idea of shopping. Regardless of where one falls in this arena, one usually has a place or a product, a venue, or an outlet that in some way satisfies the shopping urge. If you will not go to Costco on a Saturday, chances are there is some other store or place you would go to in order to look at, browse, or buy. Whether that is good or bad, whether it marks the spiritual bankruptcy of our culture or the moral waning of what we see as right or wrong, people do it for a variety of reasons. This book is about how shopping has come to be a full-fledged leisure activity and a very prominent entertainment experience.

In chapter one, the magical and almost ethereal feelings that many shoppers experience are discussed, within the context of sense of space. The environment of shopping as an entertainment experience is a key reason—some one might argue the main reason—for the experience of awe and fantasy. The second chapter in this work begins by exploring the myriad ways in which shopping has evolved into a combination of leisure and entertainment. Focus is placed on an analysis of the spectacle that has become shopping. As well, defining both entertainment and leisure suggest that shopping is in fact a significant element of the entertainment process. The history of the department store is discussed in chapter three, with specific reference made to its entertainment role. Its status as a surrogate for the theater, museum and gallery as well as a cathedral is also discussed. Department stores were often at the forefront of shopping as an entertainment experience, utilizing fashion shows and shop windows in their attempts to entice customers.

Chapter four deals with the mall—the definitive post modern entertainment experience. From its rather humble origins to its most sophisticated manifestations, the mall has replaced the circus and the carnival to become the most entertaining of all shopping venues. A more hyper-attuned version of this last point is to be located within the realm of the E-Store or entertainment store with its hyper-stimulating array of lights, screens, and special effects, the subject of chapter five. This relatively recent phenomenon has merged all that modern technology has to offer with the traditional notion of shopping. On the one hand there is the high technology foundation but traditional offerings also abound. Shopping has become serious and vital to many people in the West. Regardless what critics think and feel, chapter six deals with the idea that people embrace shopping as a leisure activity and entertainment outlet that provides them with a huge psychological boost. Not only is this happening, but it is occurring in a significant manner.

One way that shopping has embedded itself into the fabric of the entertainment economy has been as a surrogate for *edutainment*. The world of Ralph Lauren, analyzed in chapter seven, is a world where dreams can come alive, but one that also teaches, even in a marginal way. The Lauren universe has been capable of transcending need and want and has also allowed people to live and wear what they see and desire. The final chapter is oriented around the fact that museums and galleries throughout the world all offer a wide array of goods to visitors. Once this activity was marginal to the structure of the institution; now it is a significant element of most cultural institutions. A *New Yorker* cartoon, drawn by Jason Patterson, in the July 24, 2006, issue has one small building, labeled "Museum of Commerce" with a much larger building beside it with the sign "Gift Shop." The question to consider is, is this a problem? By accessing the interior and exposing the cultural capital of the museum to many, does this lessen or cheapen what is inside? Is this process, then, just the inevitable result of shopping as an entertainment experience? One answer[1] is found in another *New Yorker* cartoon, from 2001. In it the man says to the woman, as both admire a display of souvenirs, "He was such a great artist, yet in his own lifetime he never sold a single mug."

This work is about shopping as an entertainment experience. Although extremely linked to historical discourses on and of shopping, it is not a history of shopping. One of the concerns about this approach is that the work does not deal with the nefarious consequences of shopping. There are no discussions of rampant credit card debt or the paucity of purchasing salvation through acquiring consumer goods. Although I touch upon elements that are of concern, virtually no space is dedicated to a critical approach to shopping. This task remark remains the subject of and for another book. As well, I do not deal at length with the increasing dominance of the world wide web and the phenomenon of online purchasing, nor do I focus on the shopping channels found on television. What I have attempted to do is describe what is happening in this realm, hence the focus. People are doing it—as they admit in the survey information and answers to questions I have put to them—in stores, outside of malls and at dinner parties, all of which are scattered throughout the text. This acknowledgment stands alone.

NOTES

1. Thanks to Professor Robert McConkey for pointing out this cartoon.

Introduction

Not only is shopping melting into everything, but everything is melting into shopping. Through successive waves of expansion—each more extensive and pervasive than the previous—shopping has methodically encroached on a widening spectrum of territories so that it is now, arguably, the defining activity of public life. Why has it become such a basic aspect of our existence?[1]

One significant reason for the ever-widening appeal of shopping and the pervasiveness of the shopping ethos is its role as an entertainment preference. Since the middle of the nineteenth century, the act of shopping has increasingly involved much more than simply the purchasing of goods and services. From its modern manifestation in the arcades and the department store to the overwhelming atmosphere of the mall, the notion of shopping, especially in its contemporary sense, has come to be an activity of leisure and entertainment that is as important and popular as going to a movie, having dinner out, or simply strolling in a park.[2] Shopping has only increased as a viable entertainment activity in the preceding three decades. An array of organizations and institutions, designers and retailers, manufacturers and marketers have made contributions to this new form of activity. Lizabeth Cohen writes that in this new sphere of commerce, the shopping center, consuming and leisure became "inseparably intertwined."[3] According to a special issue of *Consumer Reports*, more than a third of those surveyed said that they considered shopping their hobby.[4] Shopping is now ranked as a primary leisure activity.[5] "Shopping at the mall," according to Gordon S. Wood, "now seems to be the American way of life."[6]

Although not necessarily confined to Americans, what this means is that people go to the mall just as often, if not more so, than doing anything else. Going out has become synonymous with going shopping or going to the mall. Americans, according to *The Economist*, spend more time in malls, than in any other place. With the exception of eating, sleeping, working, or watching television, going to the mall is the dominant leisure activity.[7] One source has even suggested that for Americans, shopping and watching television are the two favorite pastimes they indulged in.[8] The pinnacle of this is the creation of total shopping environments, such as the Bluewater complex in Kent, England. In these places, shopping and entertainment are merged in a way that captures all that entices, but what is particularly important is the fact that these are now places of enchantment and even re-enchantment with the world. Specifically, people find themselves in states of pleasure, comfort and satisfaction when they are shopping. Rightly or wrongly, many people now seem to get more out of purchasing goods and perusing a shopping environment than going for a walk or seeing a film. Bluewater, according to one critic, has everything for everyone without the problems found in traditional venues. It is a *"utopia"* for shopping as an entertainment, as well as a leisure experience that totally captures the synthesis of the two indulgences.[9] Shopping, as this work suggests, has become a significant entertainment component.

One indicator of how popular shopping has become as a "thing to do" is its representation in the mass media. Television has come a long way since *The Price is Right*. On the popular series *Sex and the City*, shopping occupied a substantial amount of space in the story and plot lines. Going shopping or meeting at a particular store was part of the equation. In films, numerous movies are situated around the mall or in a specific retail establishment. From *Mall Rats* to *Scenes from a Mall*, the orientation is around shopping as a form of accepted entertainment. The magazine *Lucky* is completely about shopping. This imprint devoted to shopping has become extremely popular since its launch in 2000, and now has nearly one million subscribers. Other new magazines devoted to the category are also coming out. These include *Cargo* and *Vitals*, both aimed at men, as well as *Domino* and *Wish*.[10] Rap songs include mention of numerous consumer products and brand names that one must have to define identity. The Internet is dominated by shopping and purchasing; from e-Bay to Amazon, twenty-four-seven accommodation is present. Shopping networks broadcast shows which feature merchandise that is available for sale—from the utilitarian to the sophisticated.

"I'll meet you at the Mall," "I'm going to Borders/Indigo for a few hours," "Let's go shopping," are all familiar phrases that illustrate the fact that shopping is a leisure activity that provides entertainment value to many. Many people plan their weekends around shopping. Some of the more sophisticated will meet at a market, have a coffee and peruse the more eclectic stores. Others cannot wait to get to the larger suburban shopping factories and run their carts up and down the aisles of Costco or Home Depot. Journalist Susan Sampson compares these outings to hunting and gathering expeditions.[11] This latter type of entertainment consumption is oriented around getting a bargain, which has enormous appeal to many people and becomes exceedingly satisfying. The same principles at work at getting a deal at a flea market or a garage sale seem to kick in on the factory outlet circuit. It is thrilling and exciting and can, for some, be fun.[12] Many people plan their leisure time around activities that are full-fledged shopping experiences.[13]

A department store in Toronto is launching a new brand of cosmetics. Invitations are sent out to thousands of women. The evening launch comes complete with wine and cheese. It becomes a much-sought-after engagement. On the same night, an exclusive men's wear store is holding a session on how to dress for success in business. Representatives from a number of manufacturers will be there giving talks. The evening finishes with malt scotch and cigars. It is a big success and is reported in the paper the next day. Many men and women look forward to these activities and see them as forms of excursion, as entertainment possibilities that are just as satisfying as any definition of "a night out." Yet both are intimately linked to shopping.

Thomas Hine feels that the significance of shopping is so pervasive that he has coined the term "buyosphere" to describe this realm. What Hine means by the "buyosphere" is that the popularity of shopping and all of its manifestations, encompassing "physical and virtual places" also extends to a unique "state of mind." Hine suggests that this goes beyond stores and must include everything from Web sites to fashion magazines.[14]

Shopping in its modern sense is intimately connected to the rise of leisure. For the majority of people, it was after the middle ages and during the Renaissance that leisure and entertainment first became codified. The ability to think above the fundamentals of life and to move beyond mere subsistence came with more stability and a better economy. The creation of shopping as a full-fledged entertainment experience is a postmodern phenomenon. But it is important to recognize that shopping always carried with it entertainment elements. Whether bartering in Mesopotamia or buying in a Flanders trade fair, elements of suspense and entertainment, action and pleasure have always been part of the equation. As Laura Byrne Paquet has observed, "The stage today is bigger and better lit, but the process modern marketers call 'the retail drama' has been going on for centuries."[15]

Shopping, according to this interpretation, is predicated on the rise of leisure, which in turn has merged with the unleashing of consumption from its traditional parameters. Leisure, according to Michael Marrus, is defined as "a free activity, which an individual engages in for his own purposes, whatever these may be."[16] Historically, consumption or shopping was heavily regulated as an activity and the sites where and times when consumers engaged in the process of shopping were quite circumscribed.[17] In Toronto, for example, until quite recently one could not shop on a Sunday.

A seminal event in the history of shopping as an entertainment experience occurred in 1947. In the United States, shortly after the Second World War, modern consumer society, which had long been curtailed, by both the Depression and the sacrifices imposed during the war, was ready to pursue shopping in a significant way. Central to this process was the design of stores. At a trade show held in New York City, retailers recognized and "asserted" that the key to "entrancing" customers was to make shopping as entertaining as possible. Shopping thus became firmly equated with an exceptional entertainment experience. According to M. Jeffrey Hardwick, newspapers wrote about the openings of certain stores, Grayson's in particular, "as if they were Broadway openings." Hardwick relates that in a number of cases, "articles even went so far as to acknowledge that perhaps shopping in the new environments was even more fun than seeing a show."[18]

It is virtually impossible to conceive of the Western world without some reference to an activity related to shopping. From the Greek agora, to the shops of the Roman Forum to the medieval fair, the act of buying and selling has occupied a central role in the social and cultural activities of Western culture.[19] Shopping, even in its nascent form was always an active and social activity. Rome and many of the cities within its empire boasted thriving shops and markets, hawkers and shopkeepers galore, all adding up to a remarkably dynamic atmosphere. Andrew Dalby writes, "The traffic and the trade in the streets of central Rome competed for every inch of space. Shops had crowded on to the pavements, wine-jars were chained to the base of columns . . ."[20] The medieval trade fair or its larger cousin, the regional fair, provided vital space for social interaction in the cities that remained standing during this era, and later, the markets played a crucial role in the revitalization of cities.

Jennifer Jones, building on the ideas of Jurgen Habermas, has suggested that during the later part of the eighteenth century, the increased availability of consumer goods spurred on the notion of what constitutes shopping. In turn, it became an integral part of public-sphere activity. As Jones writes, there was an entertainment quality to shopping even at this stage. "Part of the fun of shopping for the upper classes," she writes, "was the opportunity to be out in society and feel a la mode. One went shopping not merely to purchase clothing or accessories but to buy where all the rest of fashionable society was currently buying."[21] Classes did mingle in many shopping environments. For many in the middle-class echelon, the ability to handle or buy what was once the preserve of the elite, especially within the elegant new department stores, only added to the sense of excitement.

Although there are numerous exceptions, it is documented that prior to the 1840s, most people simply bargained for and bought what they needed—if one could not produce the object for them.[22] One of the key features that distinguish shopping from the act of buying is time. Making a purchase is one thing, but shopping requires time. It becomes a leisure activity when the time spent is unhurried. Shopping means looking, visualizing, and caressing. As Anne Friedberg has astutely recognized, shopping is also more about desire than need. Friedberg writes, "To shop is to muse in the contemplative mode, an activity that combines diversion, self-gratification, expertise, and physical activity."[23]

Historically, the market was a place of freedom for women, but also, it served as an environment where one could catch up on the latest gossip, speak to relatives and neighbors, and in general, share information.[24] As well, markets were often surroundings where a variety of entertainments took place: jugglers, fire-eaters, fortunetellers, and other performers gathered at the markets. At the Sturbridge Fair in England, bear baiting, stage-comedies and playing a round of golf were offered as entertainments.[25] Not only could one shop, but entertainments also abounded, including "plays, music, and feasts." Not only could people socialize, but they could also be entertained as well as buy something to eat or drink.[26]

For a significant part of the early modern period in Europe, shopping was often considered a male form of entertainment, in which flirting was synonymous with the process of making a purchase. The female merchant or shop worker was as often as much of an object of desire for the male as the merchandise.[27] Before fixed prices, which were characteristic of the department store, bargaining proved to be quite an entertaining component of the purchasing ritual. As Richard Sennet has written, "Haggling and its attendant rituals are the most ordinary instances of everyday theater in a city, and of the public man as an actor."[28] The notion of theater is an all-important trope in the spectacle of shopping. It has been a significant part of making a purchase for quite some time. Especially before the advent of the fixed price and the unstated obligation to make a purchase, the idea of haggling over the price, of bargaining, of dickering, was a significant theatrical part of the socio-entertainment process in the years before the department store freed things up. Sennet conveys that this process took a fair degree of time and discouraged rapid turnover. As well, the vendor got to know his or her customers. What the founder of the *Bon Marché* could be said to have done was invert this theatricality and move toward a form of mass spectacle. This removed the intimacy of the theatrical process and placed it more in line with the observable distance of mass entertainment.[29] Thus, the shopping mall, or the modern store itself, has a long history as an entertainment venue. The early founders of the major department stores—in France, the United States and Britain—all had this approach in mind. Their spectacular displays, luxurious trappings, fine selection of goods, and numerous leisure activities gave them an audience that almost rivaled the great cathedrals.[30]

The cathedral comparison is quite apt. It was Emile Zola's term for what was occurring within the new palaces. In *Au Bonheur Des Dames*, Zola talked about the beams and joists, the light and the air. He called the department store "a cathedral of modern trade, light yet solid, designed for a congregation of lady customers."[31] Accordingly, the department store as a cathedral replaced or even took over from religion. Appropriately,

> It had its consecrated building, and its own rituals and festive seasons in the form of designated times for sales and events in relation to particular themes and product groups: linens, toys, oriental rugs; autumn and spring fashions; winter and summer sales.[32]

The idea of the cathedral-like atmosphere of the department store carries over quite strongly into the realm of the mall or shopping center. Developers are very keenly aware that in entering a shopping center or a mall, one is entering a different kind of space. Like the grand department stores, the mall has the large spaces, which trigger a sense of awe. Utilizing height and skylights, the consumer is immersed in an environment that is fundamentally different from the everyday. There is a unique feeling when one enters these secular cathedrals and it is deliberate.[33]

The new department stores themselves became as talked about locally as did some of the large urban structures and often the major exhibitions. Going shopping in the new department stores became an experience. This experience was designed to transcend the everyday. It became, like visiting the Great Exhibition or a major tourist attraction, capable of producing a "liminal moment."[34] It was something other than what one experienced everyday; it involved a mixing of excitement and a lessening of the restrictions on normal expectations.[35] The glamour and the elegance that was part of the early department stores, complete with the ability to browse and touch, to sample the visual attractions and to be enticed by the aromas only enhanced the exceptional environment that was created. Like a living theater, it was structured around fantasy and escape, but for many, it was cost-free and safer than the vagaries of the city proper.[36]

The importance of the great exhibitions, annual fairs, and other trade expositions to the world of shopping as a form of entertainment cannot be ignored.[37] The Worlds Fairs became "engines for showcasing material culture," especially in the late nineteenth and early twentieth centuries. In most instances, these sites became places of transformation. Objects and services came to be seen as spectacles and were invested with numerous modern associations.[38] Whether it was the Chicago or New York World's Fair (which Victor Gruen worked on) or Expo '67 in Montreal, one of the seminal attributes beyond the display of new inventions and techniques was the utilization of corporate sponsorship. One of the reasons why this process is so interesting and important is that the Disney Corporation was at the forefront in engaging companies to become part of their complexes, in particular Epcot. According to Fabian Faurholt Csaba and Soren Askegaard:

> The idea is to link names and logos of major companies to exhibits and attractions and to develop cross-marketing opportunities, in which mall and partner/sponsor promote each other in and outside the mall. Exhibitions, displays and events attract media attention and consumer traffic.[39]

At key points throughout many malls, corporations display new products, from cars to new technology devices, all of which are akin to what is seen at Epcot and other amusement parks.

This process has often troubled critics and the counterculture. Never content with allowing the ethos of consumption to get too deep into the culture at large, these stalwart anti-consumption advocates have consistently launched attacks at any proponents of shopping and consumption. What has hampered this process has been the equally persistent co-optation of the so-called radical element's arsenal. Everything from clothing to attitude is quickly reworked and reproduced as something to be bought or sold, something to be accumulated. Representatives of the counterculture often work extremely hard to create their own culture, in the form of language, clothing, food and drink, only to have it repackaged and on display at Bloomingdales, before the next issue of *Adbusters* is out.[40] Harnessing elements from the environment at large has always been of great appeal to both shoppers and retailers.

The Viennese-born Victor Gruen, architect and pioneer of the mall concept, began his approach with shopping centers, which were deliberately designed to capture the spirit, the essence, and the enchanting entertainment qualities of European markets. Gruen was aware that one of the distinguishing attributes of the mall would be the community and cultural focus. Whether in the form of meeting casually or of becoming a key artistic arena, Gruen was very aware that what had made previous shopping conglomerations, such as the town square or the market, successful in Europe was their social and cultural vibrancy.[41]

The department store, the shopping arcade, the market, the shopping center, and the mall became magnets for attracting people from virtually all walks of life (although many were structured and segregated along specific class lines), who were brought in and compelled to come for more than just the purchase of a luxury or a necessity. The social and, importantly, the entertainment element to these places of consumption quickly surpassed the prosaic realities of everyday buying.

People came to the department store—and still do—for more than simply the purchase of a good or service. They met there, had lunch, a drink, and spent the day. In the late 1970s and throughout the 1980s, Bloomingdale's marketed itself as the social center for the hip and the young. On Saturday mornings, the Lexington Avenue store was packed with trendy singles, as well as celebrities hanging out at *the* place to be and be seen.[42] Many people gravitate toward shopping venues in order to both meet and to see other people. It has even been suggested that the new place to meet people, rather than go through a dating service, is at the large bookstores, such as Barnes and Noble. The social and voyeuristic opportunities provided by stores are appealing to many individuals. It has become chic, vogue, and cool to hang out in stores, to peruse the aisles and to simply, 'just go.'

Importantly, shopping is now an endeavor that people can do in their free time, something to fall back on as a leisure activity. It is accepted as an appropriate diversion or entertainment activity, akin to going to a movie or taking a walk is. This is not something that those critical of rampant consumerism are at all comfortable with; nonetheless, it is a significant activity for many. Naomi Klein criticizes the rampant consumerism inherent in "logo" culture, complete with the nefarious attempts of corporations to produce their products as cheaply as possible.[43] The authors of the book *Affluenza* discuss the fact that Americans spend trillions of dollars on consumer goods every year, and have twice as many shopping centers as high schools. They cite statistics suggesting that shopping is something that people do instead of, for example, playing with children. Consequently, going to the mall is seen as natural.[44] Many critics on the left are uncomfortable with their dependence on shopping as an entertainment activity. A letter to style columnist Heather Mallick criticized her for attempting to espouse "socialist" values while at the same time glorifying her love of shopping. In her response, she wrote, "The message is that socialists shouldn't buy nice things. It's almost as bad as another conservative article of faith, that feminists should be ugly."[45]

It is important to state and to recognize that in the Western world, especially in the United States, the freedom to shop is deemed incredibly important, which ties in with the triumph of commercial culture. In a century that held two bloody world wars and saw the rise and fall of communism in the Soviet Union, as well as a modified communism that embraced capitalism, the fact is that of all the "isms" to compete, consumerism has been victorious.[46] Challenges have been numerous and effective, tenaciously fought and thoughtfully articulated, but despite it all, the ethos of consumerism held on. "Consumerism," is defined as "the belief that goods give meaning to individuals and their roles in society."[47] As Gary Cross has recognized, despite not having a platform, or leaders, consumerism dominated and triumphed because it was aligned to individualism, liberty, and democracy. It was also something virtually every newcomer could embrace and relate to. Consumerism could transcend the class structure of Europe and could be embodied in and with real social needs. If freedom of expression is a central tenet of the American way of life, the freedom to shop and to enjoy shopping is readily embraced.[48]

Shopping has also come to play a vital motivational role in travel. The similarities between shopping and travel, in particular, their pleasurable characteristics, are closely related. Both of these experiences occur outside of the home, and have a liminal element to them in that they happen somewhere out of the ordinary.[49] This is especially pronounced in the new tourist shopping destinations, whether the Mall of America or in Las Vegas or Dubai, something unexpected and otherworldly is going on.

Most tourists and many travelers are aware of the shopping district(s) in the places they are visiting. Virtually everyone who has traveled somewhere can name the main shopping street (Fifth Avenue, Michigan Avenue, the Champs Elysees) and has an intimate knowledge of some famous store or series of shops. Upon their return, they are as likely to be asked if they had been to Nanjing road as some historic monument or museum. In a culture that equates shopping with entertainment, and increasingly, with culture and education, this is part of the evolution.

In the progression from travel to tourism it is important to recognize that some tangible manifestation of this experience had to be documented. The rise of "markers" for having been there, such as artwork or the ubiquitous T-shirt, serve to remind both those who have traveled and those who have not, that person X was away.[50] The third often cited reason for travel to New York is to shop.[51] Many guidebooks devote substantial space to shopping in foreign cities and attempt to suggest the best in consumption that a place has to offer.

Apparently, this process amuses locals. As Susan Willis relates, people who live in Maine, close to the famous L.L. Bean store, which has become a magnet for tourists, spend time watching families arrive and shop at all hours. This, she terms, "consumer tourism."[52] People are increasingly traveling to shop, which takes the notion of the souvenir to a whole new level. Unlike the medieval pilgrims who traveled far to visit a shrine and maybe purchase a mirror or a badge with the picture of a saint,[53] these tourists are motivated by the reverse. Planeloads of travelers are now whisked to destinations simply for the purpose of shopping. Both the Mall of America and the West Edmonton Mall are focal points in the constellation of consumer tourism.

The definitive example of the important role that shopping plays as an entertainment experience is most probably, the West Edmonton Mall or WEM. As Tracy Davis writes,

> Since its completion in 1985, the Mall has become a leisure centre for millions of suburbanites and tourists attracted by the world's largest indoor amusement park, the world's largest indoor golf course, the world's largest indoor wave pool, the only landlocked full-size replica of the Santa Maria, a larger fleet of operable submarines than in the Canadian Navy, and nearly 1000 stores and services.[54]

The WEM, by evolving into one of the most popular tourist attractions in Canada, is the ultimate manifestation of the fusing of shopping, entertainment and leisure. The fusion of shopping with leisure and entertainment and vice versa, has a recent history that can be summed up in one word: Disneyfication. This idea suggests that shopping, entertainment and leisure can be rolled into one concept: that of the theme park. The notion of themes derives from Disney's emphasis on merchandising in the most friendly and non-threatening of surroundings, but has evolved into elaborate, even fantastical total environments. Today, this can run the gamut from restaurants like the Hard Rock Café to environments such as Playdium. Participation is encouraged not just by purchasing and consuming, but also by being part of the aggregate surroundings.[55] What often occurs in this blurring of boundaries is the deliberate creation of what Guy Julier has termed "retail-tainment sites."[56]

The principal extension of this is the entertainment stores or 'E-stores,' such as Niketown or The Warner Bros. Stores. People gravitate toward these environments to spend time but also to buy products. Like Niketown in Chicago, Ralph Lauren's store in the Rhinelander Mansion in New York City has become a must-visit site when in Manhattan. As Jeffrey Tractenberg has written, although they were not buying, customers at the Ralph Lauren store "looked happier than many leaving nearby $7-a-ticket movie theaters. Here admission was free. If nothing else, the entertainment value was outstanding."[57] When these structures start to become tourist destinations and "must-see" places, such as some large and fancy supermarket, the dialectic is complete. No longer are you simply just shopping for food, a basic human situation, but now one must sample the most exotic foods from all over the world in an atmosphere that rivals the museum. Dean & Deluca, Zabar's, Fortnum & Mason, and their equivalents all over the Western world are often described in detail in many guidebooks as if they are on par with certain museums. For the culinary consumer/traveler, they may in fact surpass what the museum holds. A "pilgrimage" made to these places carries the same expectations as a holy site. Tourists, complete with guidebooks, stand in line outside Parisian bakeries, to sample bread or some other creation, in order to see if author Adam Gopnick was right in writing about the delicacies available.

It is possible to shop in virtually every space conceivable. Airports have evolved into mini-malls that are just as popular as downtown avenues and suburban malls. Many of the finest retail establishments occupy airport concourses and provide travelers with opportunities to occupy their time.[58] Many large hotels, especially the more luxurious ones, have shops, and even malls, for guests to indulge in their shopping urges.[59] Cruise ships now have considerable shopping options available for their passengers. The fact that they hold a captive audience combined with the willingness to shop on vacation means that stores are going to be on the sea as well.[60]

This synergy is also known as "shoppertainment." This merging of the entertainment qualities of mass media with the retail experience in an often-recreated "biosphere" provides a nonstop accent of "bells and whistles" that shoppers have to ring and blow. Within stores, there is no shortage of opportunities to have this kind of "fun." From DJs playing music, to television screens, to sporting activities, amusements abound.[61] The grocery store or the supermarket is also a place where this process occurs. Lighting and staging are used to enhance the appeal of produce; props and sets are employed to accent what would otherwise be dismissed as prosaic. Suddenly, going to the supermarket takes on an air of adventure and entertainment; a theatrical element invades and creates an aura of exoticism and excitement.[62] "When I have time," states one respondent, "I love to go up and down the aisles, looking at things, reading the labels, comparing different products. It's enjoyable. It's fun. Especially at the new Loblaws. I find their store design upscale and appealing." In order to compete with the various alternatives available for leisure and entertainment, shopping has had to move into the entertainment field in a significant way.[63]

The notion of shopping and consumption as a form of entertainment is enhanced by the production of items that are in essence public relations tools, which reinforce the idea of shopping as an entertainment experience. A significant trend in the past few years that illustrates this phenomenon has been the rise of glossy corporate product magazines, that masquerade as information media but that are, in reality, slick catalogues for various products. Like the ultimate in mass leisure provided by *People* and *In Style*, Sony, Benetton, Mercedes Benz, and other corporations mix advertising into a very sophisticated entertainment formula. A related element to this fusion has been the mania for collecting shopping bags. This fad has come complete with three or four highly polished coffee-table books, which legitimize the shopping bag *as* art. Newspapers have shopping columns and profile new products. The weekend *Toronto Star* others a whole section devoted to shopping.

In the last twenty years shopping has proliferated into more than an accoutrement to one's daily activities. It has become a central feature of leisure and one that permeates all facets of life in the West and has blended and morphed into a composition of relaxation and pleasure.

NOTES

1. Sze Tsung Leong, ". . . And Then There Was Shopping," in *Harvard Design School Guide to Shopping, Project on The City 2*, directed by Rem Koolhaas (New York: Taschen, 2001), 129.

2. Juliet Schor, *The Overworked American: The Unexpected Decline of Leisure* (New York: Basic Books, 1991), 107.

3. Lizabeth Cohen, *A Consumer's Republic: The Politics of Mass Consumption in Postwar America* (New York: Knopf, 2003), 270.

4. James B. Twitchell, *Lead Us Into Temptation: The Triumph of American Materialism* (New York: Columbia University Press, 1999), 245.

5. Stefan Theil, "The Fine Art of Shopping," *Newsweek*, International Edition (October 28, 2002), 86.

6. Gordon S. Wood, "The Shopper's Revolution," *The New York Review of Books*, (June 10, 2004), 26.

7. Cited in Bill Bryson, *Made In America: An Informal History of the English Language in the United States* (New York: William Morrow and Co., 1994), 217–18.

8. Cited in William Green, *The Retail Store: Design and Construction* (San Jose, Calif./New York: iUniverse.com, Inc., 2001), ix.

9. Iain Borden, "Fashioning the City: Architectural Tactics and Identity Statements," *Architectural Design: Fashion and Architecture* 70, no. 6 (December 2000): 14.

10. Deborah Fulsang, "Shop Till You Drop," *The Globe and Mail* (August 14, 2004), L4.

11. Susan Sampson, "Thinking inside the Box," *The Toronto Star* (November 5, 2003), D4.

12. Jim Pooler, *Why We Shop: Emotional Rewards and Retail Strategies* (Westport, Conn.: Praeger, 2003), 60.

13. See Sharon Zukin's personal comments in *Point of Purchase: How Shopping Changed American Culture* (New York: Routledge, 2004), 2–5.

14. Thomas Hine, *I Want That! How We All Became Shoppers* (New York: Harper Collins, 2002), xv.

15. Laura Byrne Paquet, *The Urge To Splurge: A Social History of Shopping* (Toronto: ECW Press, 2003), 13.

16. Cited in Witold Rybczynski, *Waiting for the Weekend* (New York: Viking, 1991), 118.

17. Rob Shields, "Spaces for the Subject of Consumption," in *Lifestyle Shopping: The Subject of Consumption*, ed. Rob Sheilds (New York: Routledge, 1992), 6.

18. M. Jeffrey Hardwick, *Mall Maker: Victor Gruen, Architect of an American Dream* (Philadelphia: University of Pennsylvania Press, 2004), 69.

19. Joel Kotkin, *The New Geography: How the Digital Revolution is Reshaping the American Landscape* (New York: Random House, 2000), 144, 145.

20. Andrew Dalby, *Empire of Pleasures: Luxury and Indulgence in the Roman World* (London: Routledge, 2000), 210, 221.

21. Jennifer Jones, "'Coquettes' and 'Grisettes': Women Buying and Selling in Ancien Regime Paris," in *The Sex of Things: Gender and Consumption in Historical Perspective*, eds. Victoria de Grazia with Ellen Furlough (Berkeley: University of California Press, 1996), 32, 33.

22. Susan Strasser, *Satisfaction Guaranteed: The Making of the American Mass Market* (New York: Pantheon/Random House, 1989), 15. Strasser writes, ". . . branded, standardized products came to represent the new networks and systems of production and distribution, the social relationships that brought people the things they used. Household routines involved making fewer things and purchasing more; consumption became a major part of the work of the household. Formerly *customers*, purchasing the objects of daily life from familiar craftspeople and storekeepers, Americans became *consumers*."

23. Anne Friedberg, *Window Shopping: Cinema and the Postmodern* (Berkeley: University of California Press, 1994), 57.

24. Paquet, *The Urge To Splurge*, 32.

25. Dalby, *Empire of Pleasures*, 229, and Paquet, *The Urge To Splurge*, 34.

26. Ann Satterthwaite, *Going Shopping: Consumer Choices and Community Consequences* (London: Yale University Press, 2001), 20.

27. Jones, "'Coquettes' and 'Grisettes,'" 32.

28. Richard Sennett, *The Fall of Public Man* (New York: Vintage, 1978), 142.

29. Sennett, *The Fall of Public Man*, 142–144.

30. Rita Kramer, "Cathedrals of Commerce," *City Journal* (Spring 1996), 81, 85.

31. Emile Zola, *Au Bonheur Des Dames (The Ladies' Delight)* (London: Penguin, [1883] 2001), 231.

32. Rachel Bowlby, *Carried Away: The Invention of Modern Shopping* (New York: Columbia University Press, 2001), 10.

33. Ira G. Zepp Jr., *The New Religious Image of Urban America: The Shopping Mall as Ceremonial Center*, Second Edition (Niwot: University Press of Colorado, 1997), 127.

34. See Victor Turner, *The Ritual Process: Structure and Anti-Structure* (New York: Aldine de Gruyter, 1995).

35. See Susan S. Fainstein and Dennis R. Judd, "Global Forces, Local Strategies and Urban Tourism," in *The Tourist City*, eds. Dennis R. Judd and Susan S. Fainstein (London: Yale University Press, 1999), 10.

36. Ann Satterthwaite, *Going Shopping: Consumer Choices and Community Consequences* (London: Yale University Press, 2001), 29.

37. See Keith Walden, *Becoming Modern in Toronto: The Industrial Exhibition and the Shaping of A Late Victorian Culture* (Toronto: University of Toronto Press, 1997), chap. 3.

38. Vanessa R. Schwartz and Jeannene M. Przyblyski, "Visual Culture's History," in *The Nineteenth-Century Visual Culture Reader*, eds. Vanessa R. Schwartz and Jeannene M. Przyblyski (London: Routledge, 2004), 7.

39. Gabian Faurholt Csaba and Soren Askegaard, "Malls and the Orchestration of the Shopping Experience in a Historical Perspective," *Advances in Consumer Research* vol. 26, 1999, 38.

40. See Joseph Heath and Andrew Potter, *The Rebel Sell: Why the Culture Can't Be Jammed* (Toronto: HarperCollins, 2004).

41. Satterthwaite, *Going Shopping*, 110.

42. Marvin Traub (and Tom Teicholz), *Like No Other Store: The Bloomingdale's Legend and the Revolution in American Marketing* (New York: Random House, 1993), 116–119.

43. See Naomi Klein, *No Logo: Taking Aim at the Brand Bullies* (Toronto: Knopf Canada, 2000). In an interesting irony, marketers have been using her critical text as a way to reach the generation that does not wish to be part of mainstream consumer culture.

44. John De Graaf, David Wann, and Thomas H. Naylor, *Affluenza: The All-Consuming Epidemic* (San Francisco: Berrett-Koehler Publishers, Inc., 2001), 13–14.

45. Heather Mallick, "Who Says Shopping's a Sin For a Socialist," *The Globe and Mail* (July 10, 2004), F2.

46. Gary Cross, *An All-Consuming Century: Why Commercialism Won in Modern America* (New York: Columbia University Press, 2000), 1.

47. Cross, *An All-Consuming Century*, 1.

48. Cross, *An All-Consuming Century*, 1–3.

49. Turo-Kimmo Lehtonen and Pasi Maenpaa, "Shopping in the East Centre Mall," in *The Shopping Experience*, eds. Pasi Falk and Colin Campbell (London: SAGE Publications, 1997), 146.

50. Juliet Schor, *The Overspent American: Upscaling, Downshifting and the New Consumer* (New York: Basic Books, 1998), 48.

51. Twitchell, *Lead Us Into Temptation*, 26.

52. Susan Willis, "The Family Vacation," in *Inside the Mouse: Work and Play at Disney World*, The Project on Disney (Durham: Duke University Press, 1995), 39.

53. John Man, *The Gutenberg Revolution* (London: Review, 2002), 62.

54. Tracy C. Davis, "Theatrical Antecedents of the Mall that Ate Downtown," *Journal of Popular Culture* 24, no. 4 (Spring 1991), 1.

55. Aaron Betsky, "All the World's a Store: The Spaces of Shopping," in *Brand.new*, ed. Jane Pavitt (Princeton: Princeton University Press, 2000), 135–139.

56. Guy Julier, "From Object to Experience," in *Brand.new*, ed. Jane Pavitt, 149.

57. Jeffrey A. Tractenberg, *Ralph Lauren: The Man Behind the Mystique* (Boston/Toronto: Little Brown & Co., 1988), 7, 8.

58. Michelle Lee, *Fashion Victim: Our Love-Hate Relationship with Dressing, Shopping and the Cost of Style* (New York: Broadway Books, 2003), xxiv.

59. See Pico Iyer, *The Global Soul: Jet Lag, Shopping Malls, and the Search for Home* (New York: Vintage, 2001). Throughout the book there are constant references to the fact that airport shopping areas and malls are very similar.

60. Debra Hazel, "Floating Shopping Centers?" *Shopping Centers Today* (May 2004, htttp://www.icsc.org/srch/sct/sct0504/page129.html).

61. Lee, *Fashion Victim*, 77–79.

62. Paquet, *The Urge to Splurge*, 54–55.

63. Jody Patraka,"Foreword" to *Lifestyle Stores*, Martin M. Pegler (New York: PBC International, 1996).

1

✛

Liminality, Magic, and the Pleasure of the Shopping Place

The word "magic" appears throughout this work. One reason for this has to do with the fact that this word is thrown out quite often when people are asked to describe their shopping experiences. "It was magical" is the phrase—not applied to a movie or a trip, but to visiting a store or going to a mall. The magic that is described by consumers is very similar to the feelings they experience when they do something other than the ordinary.

When a person engages in something that is different from their everyday life, whether thought or experience, a liminal moment has occurred. The phrase, coined by anthropologist Victor Turner, connotes an event of religious significance. Yet it aptly describes the emotions and experiences that individuals feel in certain shopping environments. A salient feature of Turner's idea of liminality involves the following concept. The observer or participant can look at the "ritual" from the outside and to some extent gain a sense that something very different or special is going on beyond a certain boundary. But for the liminal concept to really be experienced, one has to enter, to go inside the physical space, which can cause an altering of one's mental state. The individual has to cross over and almost willingly surrender the mundane and everyday in order for something extraordinary to happen. Although referenced in religious terms that concept is enormously relevant to shopping as an entertainment experience.[1]

Although the concept of a liminal experience could be applied to a visit to a medieval cathedral, to seeing a natural wonder, or via an extremely emotional trigger, one could make the argument that liminality can be created or initiated today in an almost artificial way. A hallmark of post-modern culture, one of its many defining characteristics is the fact that a variety of styles and themes are mixed and merged together to form a *pastiche* of multiple meanings. Unlike modernity, the postmodern "ortho-doxy" thrives on the merging of many different views and numerous dis-positions. The result can be that there is no dominant paradigm, no single "privileged perspective from which to judge." We can, as Belk and Bryce suggest, try on many things or wear many hats in an attempt to find out who we are or explore who we wish to be.[2] This results in a constant quest for newness; for novelty, for uniqueness and for difference. Within the shopping environment, this manifests itself in retailers trying to create something that a consumer may find novel and unique.

The combination of pastiche and *bricolage*, when added to the quest for new and novel, leads to attempts to recreate the fantastic, which has been described as spectacle and hyperreality. In turn, there is a tendency to show only the surface and to neglect the deeper meanings that may cause concern and trouble. Russell Belk and Wendy Bryce make the connection that consumers are like visitors to the Land of Oz, Frank L. Baum—the pi-oneer window designer's creation. The Emerald City metaphor suggests that the color green and the green glasses "which lend each object an emerald hue," evokes in contemporary terms a store's attempt to create and display "magical transformations."[3]

A substantial reason for the appeal of retail entertainment sites, e-stores, super malls, and certain shops is the often necromantic appeal that they offer to people raised on the ethos of consumerism. Whether it is the quasi-religious pilgrimage or the liminal expectations, something truly entertaining is at work for many people. In the realm of the toy store, the feelings that are generated upon visiting FAO Schwartz in New York are quite pronounced for many people. The entertainment consumption equation is further enhanced when people seek out the same experience that may have occurred as part of a plot from a Hollywood-produced film. The movie *Big* featured a famous scene that many have attempted to recreate, confirm or even just graze, by going into the once defunct, but reborn FAO Schwartz store in New York. There was *something* special about that store and many others. Numerous people have confirmed that certain stores held a special meaning for them as children and they have hoped to recapture that feeling or that association when adults. As well, many attempt to instill those same emotions in their children. According to Laurie Chang, as an adult walking through the aisles of FAO Schwartz, the feelings were particularly strong as an entertainment encounter: "The experience was just awesome—the size and all the toys you can think of. The most impressive thing was the stuffed animals seven feet tall."[4] That experience, that feeling, is very common among shoppers.

The magic of Disney [5] translates quite readily, into the experience of visiting the Disney store. Children in particular are awestruck upon seeing the array of colors, textures, patterns and lights. Adults as well are captivated by the spectacle and are entranced inside. The sophistication and nostalgic familiarity make this a very different retail environment from the old models. According to the vice president of visual merchandising for Old Navy, the little general store is gone. Merchandising

> has become entertainment: spinning signs, flashing lights, thumping music. We've got video screens, interactive computer kiosks, playhouses and day care for the kids. Some of us even offer In-store cafes, with soup and sandwiches for hungry shoppers.[6]

Paramount in this process is that fact that consumers, like viewers, willingly suspend their perceptions of reality and often enter into a world of prepackaged spectacle. The merging of the physical environment, the space, and all its trappings, together with an individual's desire to become part of the process is both unique and powerful.[7] Factors that enhance all of the above can range widely. Relationship to physical environment is one of the most potent, yet things such as memory and age also contribute to the spectacle of shopping as an entertainment environment. One of the main reasons why the rise of shopping related to the past—in the form of everything from retro stores to heritage sites—has become so popular has been because of the desire among those who are aging, to recapture the sensations, smells and feelings that they had as children. Even if these memories never existed, their Hollywood-produced triggers can be utilized and are greatly sought out.[8] One of the more tangible manifestations of this can come from the shopping environment.

Sites of consumption have always been social places and have always attracted those in search of products and stimulation. Shopping, whether in a medieval market, or in a small shop in early modern Europe, always offered forms of exhilaration that took one away from the everyday. Accordingly, on the American frontier, frequenting the general store or even receiving a mail-order catalogue came to be included as a form of amusement. Paul Glennie intimates that this form of activity was a way for settlers to be entertained. Looking at what a store had to offer opened up a consumer's mind to wonders not always available. It was energizing and enkindled the mental imagery of a society that did not readily change.[9]

One of the reasons why electronic versions of shopping, online and through home shopping networks on television do not offer the same forms of interaction and stimulation as being in a shopping place, is because of the lack of diversion and social interaction. The inability to touch and to smell, to peruse and wander, discuss and compare is either not possible or completely absent from the tactile and 'real' interactions of a store.[10]

In distinguishing the words place and space, most theorists suggest that place is the geographic sense of being in a particular locale, while space is something created or has been given meaning be a variety of factors. Places can change while space is the shell and usually remains the same.[11] The idea that space or place can be as much imagined as it is physical, is key to the creation of shopping as an entertainment experience. As people recall the past and their past experiences with certain elements of commercial culture, it is obvious that other factors creep in to round out the narrative of memory. The notion that arises is that the memory of a place or the "poetics of space" is inextricably linked to the imaginative reality of space.[12]

The "poetics" of space has come to have an enormous impact on how and why people shop and why they experience shopping as entertainment. In Evan S. Connell Jr.'s novel, *The Connoisseur*, the protagonist, Muhlbach, a middle-aged New Yorker, is on a trip to the Southwest—New Mexico. He has some time to kill and so goes shopping. More specifically, he wanders into a shop containing a variety of American/pre-Columbian artifacts. He spends an inordinate amount of time perusing a particular statue, examining the figure and growing more attracted to it. Interspersed throughout the lengthy description of Mulbach's bond to the object, are passages describing the region and snippets of historical information, which are tied to the owner of the shop. The process of this leisurely, unhurried transformation are detailed by Connell: "Muhlbach picks up the statue because Mrs. Soquel, once started, is difficult to stop. And as he studies the imperturbable figure he again feels the urge to buy it." He runs his hands over the base, moves his fingers over different parts of the artifact and in general, seems smitten with the piece. The Mayan figurine has cast a spell over him and he cannot believe that no one has purchased it. It has a power so strong that even when aspersions are cast over its authenticity, Mulbach does not care. "Well," he says, "I want to buy this. Regardless of whether or not it's authentic. I like it very much." His connection to the object keeps growing. He starts to wonder what it would be like to live in this region, to pick up and move. The weight of the place's past becomes synonymous with the old age of his statue. He has been someplace unique and now has a reminder, much more than a trinket or a souvenir.[13] The novel details Mulbach's increasing obsession with pre-Columbian art and traces his evolution from an amateur to the stature of a connoisseur. All of this from the act of purchasing a unique object within the confines of a unique place.

Where we are, both physically and often mentally, when we purchase something has a grand impact on how we perceive shopping and how we view shopping as an entertainment experience. Like the difference between reading a wonderful book and watching a fantastic movie, we do get entertainment stimulation, satisfaction, and wonder but often, in totally different ways and from totally different perspectives. Buying a book at a musty old used book store, with its dust and quiet is different than purchasing a book from a clean and well-lit superstore. According to Dave Hickey, Connell's creation is illustrative of what is called the "iconography of taste," whereas the quick and hyper activity that can occur in a shopping mall, within the confines of Las Vegas spectacle, is about the "iconography of desire." The distinguishing feature between the two, according to Hickey, is that when dealing with taste, desire does not cloud the process. By contrast, if one is motivated by a primary urge, taste cannot factor into the equation. Before one can make the definitive taste choice, one cannot be desperate, hungry, or driven by base urges. Hickey illustrates this by contrasting shopping in Sante Fe, New Mexico, with shopping in Las Vegas:

> Shopping in Santa Fe is slow; its pace is geological. The potential buyer is concerned with the authenticity of the object, its source and chaste appeal; in the case of native handicrafts, the buyer is even concerned with the blood, the genealogy, of the author, with his or her antique authenticity. Shopping in Vegas is quick. It is about spectacle, not scrutiny; about our desires, not the objects "virtue." So we respond not to the authenticity of the object, but to its persuasiveness, to the ornament, the rhetoric of design. We do not care who made the things we buy in Las Vegas; we luxuriate in the privilege of not caring.[14]

The character that Connell describes so well falls quite obviously into the realm of "taste." Somewhere in between is where many consumers are; they are *a priori* knowledgeable, and make their purchases not necessarily in a hasty manner, but after extracting components of taste and desire. Mass-produced goods such as Nike shoes, for example, straddle both ends. Although, increasingly, a large segment of the population do in fact care "who made the things." Both can contain elements of liminality and magic. Both speak to their purchasers and can initiate everything from memories to pride of ownership.

The increased use of two dominant themes in the creation of shopping environments seems to speak to the appeal of the liminal and the magical. One is the use of high-technology devices and interiors, cutting-edge in their intrinsic design. The other is completely the opposite: it is comfort and collegiality, nostalgia and memento-like, evocative of home.

Since the 1970s developers, designers, architects, and marketers have been increasingly attuned to the importance of the physical settings in displaying and moving goods. This awareness has grown to very sophisticated levels of engagement. Not since the heyday of the Grand Magasin, has so much thought been expended upon the way the place looks or how it feels to a particular set of consumers. An array of environmental psychologists and retailing specialists have increasingly devoted their attention to where people shop because of the connection between how shoppers behave and where they choose to purchase goods. Studies have been published on store atmospherics, lighting, color, and music in order to learn, primarily, what environmental factors can stimulate purchasing.[15]

The sense of "imaginative enjoyment" of products and where they can be consumed is buttressed by how much time, energy, and effort goes into the marketing of shopping as an entertainment experience. Advertising culture crosses many boundaries in its reach, and the "images" of consumer culture are virtually everywhere. They coalesce to form a powerful and almost omnipotent element in contemporary society—whether in the mall or in the glossy pages of a magazine. One could go so far as to suggest as Colin Campbell does that "people enjoy these images in much the same manner that they enjoy a novel or a film." Going into a store, just gazing or window-shopping, affords the potential purchaser an inordinate amount of pleasure. The enjoyment runs the gamut from "mentally 'trying on'" certain clothes to appreciating the store as a unique space.[16]

The definitive high-tech shopping environment is the Niketown situated in carefully chosen sites throughout major cities in the world. What is unique about Niketown is the fact that it has elevated the shopping experience to a level of fantasy and spectacle that was previously unheard of. The stores are overwhelming in their appropriation of cutting-edge displays and their use of technology. There is also a very subtle mixing of the old and new, which only makes each more potent in the cornucopia of sensations. In an incisive analysis of the flagship store, marketing professor Lisa Penaloza wrote: "Niketown provided consumers with an orchestrated, visually-oriented feast of artifacts and images. . . . "[17] In her research, Penaloza watched potential shoppers and observed their reactions. She concluded that they willingly participated in the production of meaning regarding the artifacts and merchandise and harnessed ideas in a way that was both deliberate and consensual. Consumers were guided through pathways throughout the site—Niketown—and at critical junctures throughout were awed by sophisticated displays and visuals, which often caused them to stop and stare. Unlike elite cultural environments, the products and references present in Niketown and abetted by celebrity endorsers, made the connections immediate and relevant. The use of superstar athletes, in particular Michael Jordan was an especially powerful symbol. In essence, when architecture, design, and marketing were combined in the store, in this very defined manner, this conflation created a unique relationship between consumer and retailer.[18]

Retail atmospheres that are cosmopolitan in their intentions and thoughtful in presentation elicit a variety of responses among consumers. It was stated in the introduction that the early department stores created a sense of awe among those who entered the doors of these grand emporiums. This feeling is still a primary response in certain shopping environments, especially those such as Niketown, which are carefully and selectively designed. The use of "high ceilings and larger-than-life celebrity displays" in Niketown triggers a sense of awe among consumers in a manner reminiscent of great sculptures and painting found in museums. Lisa Penaloza remarks that upon seeing a massive photograph of Michael Jordan, suspended from the air, a middle-aged couple immediately quieted down and began to speak in hushed tones.[19]

This kind of reverence is unique but implies, increasingly, that as a "consumption venue" Niketown straddles the boundaries of the store and the museum, with a touch of the cathedral sprinkled in. The museum-like atmosphere of Niketown is also accentuated by ubiquitous display cases and, according to Penaloza, customers asking sales staff if they could actually buy things, or did they have to pay admission.[20]

Among the other emotive and character states that consumers may experience upon entering and exploring an environment such as Niketown include visions of action and adventure, a desire for exploration and discovery, pleasure and, importantly, suspended disbelief.[21]

But Niketown also employs nostalgia or retro design in its stores and marketing. As will be referenced throughout this work, the utilization of the past has an enormously comforting, satisfying, and entertaining quality to shoppers. People like environments, products, and packaging that rekindles a memory or that sparks an association. Stephen Brown observes that Niketown is unique in that it beguiles the consumer with its melange of techno-retro:

> . . . Niketown is a totemic tabernacle, a mind-blowing melange of merchandise and memorabilia, retailing and religion, gallery and galleria, past and present. The facade of Nike's New York flagship is akin to an old-fashioned gymnasium, with an entrance modelled on traditional sports arena turnstiles. Inside, beyond the memento-lined foyer, lies a vast five-story atrium, its futuristic feel tastefully offset by period detailing (aged bricks, wooden floors, wireglass windows) and suspended marblesque states of Nike's Olympians, shod, clad and paid for by the magnificent marketer's munificence.[22]

Although his commentary is tinged with sarcasm, the point is that Nike and other retailers have created truly unique shopping environments. People want to see these places, wish to go through the doors, talk about them, and buy things within their walls. However, as Brown recognizes, "selling . . . is secondary to spectacle, to veneration, to reverence. . . ."[23]

Beyond the fundamental act of purchasing, it has been recognized that
in a society increasingly defined by technology and a sense of alienation,
one of the few places that people can find social interaction or, at the minimum, see other people, is in a shopping environment. Accord to Russel
Belk and Wendy Bryce,

> In a fruitless effort to escape from our increasingly privatized and frag-
> mented lives, we go to the mall to experience at least the illusion of commu-
> nity. . . . We desire to escape the electronic sterility of our homes and join a
> human community, even if it is a community in which we are anonymous ac-
> tors. Thus, even though the mall is a world of strangers, it provides the illu-
> sion of being a community, albeit a community based on shared beliefs in the
> value of consumption and the shared communion of purchasing the same
> brands.[24]

What Belk and Bryce say is very troubling to many people. The fact that
they get their social interaction in a mall, in a place devoted to consumption, is disturbing to some. But is it any less disturbing than getting one's
social interaction from frequenting a pub? Nonetheless, for anyone who
has ever been to a mall, there are those who seem to be there solely for the
purpose of being with other people. From a developer or retailer's perspective, there is the hope that these people will purchase something, but
one must recognize that the mall does serve as the transferred public
sphere. They have become the meeting places for the elderly, teenagers,
and those with young children.[25]

When the first malls were created, people began to come to them and
promenade in the way that people in Europe have always walked
through shopping districts. In some cases this was done on a Sunday,
when the stores at the time were closed, but often, families, dressed in
their finest, paraded leisurely through the trees, fountains and stores, with
their brightly lit window displays. In a suburban setting this was an especially attractive leisure option; to window shop in an environmentally
controlled place, free from crime, without the parking problem, was an intensely appealing alternative. [26]

Much of what has occurred over the past one hundred and fifty years
in the development of urban culture and later, commercial entertainment
culture, had to be learned and acquired by consumers. From small clusters of densely packed people, cities evolved into very different environments. Hand in hand with the growth of the modern urban metropolis, a
key development in the rise of shopping as an entertainment experience
was the conflation of the city as a shopping Mecca. The city became inextricably linked with the consumption of leisure and the move to make
shopping a full-fledged entertainment experience.[27] In contrast to rural

environments, cities have always been exciting places, filled with people and places that one would never see in the country. Cities quickly became magnets of excitement, complete with wonders that predominantly rural folk had never seen or experienced. From large and opulent buildings—architectural marvels, to electric lights and trains, from entertainment gatherings with unheard of audiences, to technological wonders such as the first cinemas and other visual and aural devices, the city offered something truly unique. Stores offered merchandise in quantities and varieties that were unheard of. They displayed goods in ways that were often incomprehensible to people fresh from the farms. And the emporiums themselves were incomparable to the local merchants' offerings. This stimulating visual spectacle was, alone, grandly appealing to visitors. Yet in order to enhance the draw of stores, something more was necessary in order to acclimatize and instruct, to familiarize and thrill.

What could make the modern city even more appealing was something unique that would draw tourists and travelers in sizes that were truly large. When major events combined elements of shopping, the process was, in many cases, almost pedagogic. Pamela Klaffke relates how the Great Exhibition of 1851 served to "foreshadow" the changes that were coming in both shopping habits and consumer behavior. The Exhibition was a consumer paradise because "the event introduced visitors to the concept of browsing and exposed them to a plethora of merchandise, carefully grouped, displayed, and free to touch—much like the experience everyday shoppers would soon have in local stores.[28]

The great exhibitions, expositions and worlds fairs, were definitive public spectacles that introduced people to products, inventions and ideas that in many cases were fundamentally new. From machines to ready-made foods, to corporate theatre, they enthralled visitors and consumers with the novel and the convenient, the rare and the mass-produced.[29]

The similarities between the contemporary shopping experience and the array of splendors afforded through the great exhibitions have grown considerably. They share an emphasis on the grand scale and technological virtuosity. In the brochure for Minnesota's Mall of America, the description of the size reads like many descriptions of visitors' accounts to worlds fairs. The literature states that the Mall of America is "as big as eighty-eight football fields, can contain twenty of Rome's St. Peter's Basilicas and is five times as large as the famous Red Square in Moscow."[30] In E. L. Doctorow's novel, *World's Fair*, size is a factor: "Even from the elevated station I could see the famous Trylon and Perisphere. They were enormous." Yet things could also be reversed and inverted; scale and simulation can be powerful. Dioramas and miniatures could overwhelm:

> Everywhere at the World's Fair the world was reduced to tiny size by the cunning and ingenuity of builders and engineers. And then things loomed up that were larger than they ought to have been."[31]

Doctorow's fictional account mentions the General Motors pavilion in the glowing terms of a child enthralled by the attempts to portray the future. He describes other corporations and their products as elements of corporate theater. A sense of wonder and hope arises, and it is inspired by place.

Many malls are also infused with themes or linkages to places and contain a variety of geographic reference points. One of the most potent aspects of place is situation. Geography and a recreated sense of place can combine to enhance a visitor's experience. One often overhears "it is just like in London" or Germany or some other destination. The simple definition of a retail store as an outlet or as "a place for storing products before customers decide to purchase them" is not only invalid but neglects the sophisticated and even passionate emotions triggered by the retail place. Successful retail environments actuate fervor within the consumer, to purchase. But that is only part of the process.[32]

Entering a place so different and so singular from what one experiences on a mundane level has a grand impact on the individual and on the consumer. Whether it is a fantastic environment such as at Disneyland, or a subdued but powerful place, such as a medieval cathedral, the impact is overwhelming. It is overwhelming in numerous ways. Pauline Maclaran and Lorna Stevens have formulated that in an instance of a consumer entering a particular shopping environment, melded out of history, "we're on the threshold of a dream. Like Alice we've passed through the looking glass . . . " This "consumer wonderland" is at one and the same time a "space full of hope," where longing, desire, and promise merge together. In essence, one has entered the equivalent of a "spectator's paradise," where history, design, and people mix together. We are, they write of this particular mall, in a piazza in Italy, a square in Holland, and an American diner.[33] This environment, as J. C. Agnew has observed, is the ultimate fusing of theater and marketplace.[34]

In the early 1990s, Caesar's Palace, the Las Vegas casino, which already had a selection of high-end stores dotting the areas not devoted to gaming, opened the Forum Shops. One of the most significant results of this gaudy, yet at the same time, opulent mall, was the fact that it was unlike any other shopping environment. Its uniqueness literally awed spectators and consumers and its impact on the move to shopping places being incommensurable atmospheres was truly revolutionary. Not only was the mall covered in marble and decorated in Roman architectural styles, but like Disney World it had animatronic talking statues and was one of the first places to have a ceiling that changed from day to night, on the half hour. For those who saw it, it was mesmerizing and attractive in a previously unheard of series of ways. What this shopping place had become was a live drama, where people literally came just to see and say that they had been there. The designer of the Forum Shops was quite specific in his intentions. It had to "be theatrical enough to compete with fantasies on film."[35]

The environments created become unreal, real places. They are places to dream, places to play, places to go to in order to get in touch, to connect, to indulge, and to fantasize. The bookstore, especially the large-scale chain has usurped the public library as a storehouse of knowledge. The library itself has had to borrow from the big bookstore to retain its uniqueness. New libraries, both public and university, take on characteristics that have been greatly influenced by entertaining bookstores. Large open spaces, murals and sculptures, fountains and coffee bars, not to forget interactive displays, computer terminals, DVD rentals and a host of magazines, all combine to make it difficult to distinguish the two.

Retail spaces can also take on more sophisticated meanings. The concept of place can be used to instruct as is the case of Japanese department stores. Not only have they been barometers of taste and fashion, but as well a sense of national cohesion and patriotic attachment can be attached to their wares.[36] To some extent, this could be said of Harrods or a selection of French department stores as well. Space—and place—can command people to act in certain ways. As architects have known for centuries, grand and large spaces inspire certain emotions, while lighting and design within can trigger other forms of behavior. The retail stage can be used for performance, drama, or emotion-filled response. Displays accent the design and the importance of the ritual of purchase takes on various levels of illusion.

The ritual of the purchase is important in harnessing and explaining the magic of shopping and the liminal experience that shoppers are prone to undergo. The overwhelming sensation of quantity and choice is a key attribute in this context. Shoppers are often dreaming of what to buy or what to possess. They wish to play with merchandise and even fantasize about what it would be like to have an abundance of certain material goods. In the actual ritual, there could be perusal, research, and even testing and trying on of a particular good. It is not just about having or buying, for within the ritual and drama the elements of amusement and entertainment are key.[37]

NOTES

1. See Victor Turner, *The Ritual Process: Structure and Anti-Structure* (New York: Aldine de Gruyter, 1995), vi, 95, and Victor Turner, "Variations on a Theme of Liminality," in *Secular Ritual*, ed. Sally F. Moore and Barbara G. Myerhoff (Assen: Van Gorcum, 1977), 37–47.

2. Russel W. Belk and Wendy Bryce, "Christmas Shopping Scenes: From Modern Miracle to Postmodern Mall," *International Journal of Research in Marketing* 10, no. 3 (1993): 278.

3. Belk and Bryce, "Christmas Shopping Scenes," 278.

4. Cited in E. McKinley, "Remembering When FAO Schwarz was Kid Heaven," *Shopping Centers Today*, February 2004, http://www.icsc.org/srch/sct/sct0203/page56.html.

5. See Walt Disney Co., *Imagineering: A Behind the Dreams Look at Making the Magic Real*, foreword by Michael D. Eisner (New York: Hyperion, 1996).

6. Jody Patraka, "Foreword," to *Lifestyle Stores*, Martin M. Pegler (New York: PBC/Rizzoli, 1996).

7. Lisa Penaloza, "Just Doing It: A Visual Ethnographic Study of Spectacular Consumption Behavior at Niketown," *Consumption, Markets and Culture* 2, no. 4 (1999): 349.

8. Stephen Brown, "Retro-Marketing: Yesterday's Tomorrows, Today!" *Marketing Intelligence & Planning* 17, no. 7 (1999): 365.

9. Paul Glennie, "Consumption within Historical Studies," in *Acknowledging Consumption*, ed. Daniel Miller (London: Routledge, 1996), 188.

10. See Gary Gumpert and Susan J. Drucker, "From the Agora to the Electronic Shopping Mall," *Critical Studies in Mass Communication*, vol. 9 (1992): 186.

11. See Michel De Certeau, *The Practice of Everyday Life* (Berkeley: University of California Press, 1984).

12. See Gaston Bachelard, *The Poetics of Space* (Boston: Beacon Press, 1964).

13. Evan S. Connell Jr., *The Connoisseur* (New York: Knopf, 1974), 4–14.

14. Dave Hickey, "Dialectical Utopias: On Santa Fe and Las Vegas," *Harvard Design Magazine*, no. 4 (Winter/Spring 1998): 4.

15. Veronique Aubert-Gamet and Bernard Cova, "Servicescapes: From Modern Non-Places to Postmodern Common Places," *Journal of Business Research*, vol. 44 (1999): 38.

16. Colin Campbell, *The Romantic Ethic and the Spirit of Modern Consumption* (Oxford: Basil Blackwell, 1987), 92.

17. Penaloza, "Just Doing It," 340.

18. Penaloza, "Just Doing It," 341.

19. Penaloza, "Just Doing It," 341, 365.

20. Penaloza, "Just Doing It," 341.

21. Penaloza, "Just Doing It," 341, 342.

22. Stephen Brown, *Marketing: The Retro Revolution* (London: Sage, 2001), 135.

23. Brown, *Marketing Intelligence and Planning*, 136.

24. Russel W. Belk and Wendy Bryce, "Christmas Shopping Scenes," *International Journal of Research in Marketing*, 10, no. 3 (1993): 293, cited in Aubert-Gamet and Cova, "Servicescapes," 41.

25. Cited in Veronique Aubert-Gamet and Bernard Cova, "Servicescapes: From Modern Non-Places to Postmodern Common Places," *Journal of Business Research*, vol. 44 (1999): 38.

26. Laura Rowley, *On Target: How The World's Hottest Retailer Hit a Bull's-Eye* (Hoboken, N.J.: Wiley & Sons, 2003), 111.

27. Geoffrey Crossick and Serge Jaumain, "The World of the Department Store: Distribution, Culture and Social Exchange," in *Cathedrals of Consumption: The European Department Store, 1850–1939*, eds. Geoffrey Crossick and Serge Jaumain (Aldershot: Ashgate, 1999), 21–25.

28. Pamela Klaffke, *Spree: A Cultural History of Shopping* (Vancouver, B.C.: Arsenal Pulp Press, 2003), 27.

29. See Robert W. Rydell, *World of Fairs: The Century of Progress Expositions* (Chicago: University of Chicago Press, 1993).

30. Cited in Mark Gottdeiner, "The Semiotics of Consumer Spaces," in John F. Sherry Jr., ed., *Servicescapes: The Concept of Place in Contemporary Markets* (Chicago: NTC Business Books, 1998), 39.

31. E. L. Doctorow, *World's Fair* (New York: Random House, 1985), 250, 254.

32. Melanie Wallendorf, Joan Lindsey-Mullikin, and Ron Pimentel, "Gorilla Marketing: Customer Animation and Regional Embeddedness of a Toy Store Servicescape," in *Servicescapes*, ed. John Sherry, Jr., 154.

33. Pauline Maclaran and Lorna Stevens, "Romancing the Utopian Marketplace," in *Romancing the Market*, ed. Stephen Brown, Anne Marie Doherty, and Bill Clare (London: Routledge, 1998), 178.

34. J. C. Agnew, cited in Maclaran and Stevens, "Romancing the Utopian Marketplace," 178.

35. Donald Shillingburg, "Entertainment Drives Retail," *Architectural Record* (August 1994): 85.

36. See Millie Creighton, "The Seed of Creative Lifestyle Shopping: Wrapping Consumerism in Japanese Store Layouts," in *Servicescapes*, ed. John F. Sherry, Jr., 201–203.

37. Mary Ann McGrath, "Dream On: Projections of an Ideal Servicescape," in *Servicescapes: The Concept of Place in Contemporary Markets*, ed. John F. Sherry Jr., 448–450.

2

+

Shopping, Leisure, and the Spectacle of Entertainment

Shopping as an entertainment experience is predicated on the rise of leisure and the pursuit of entertainment outlets. Simply put, once people had the time to engage in activities other than work and once they had become accustomed to viewing and participating in entertainment outlets, it would not take much time for them to incorporate shopping into their entertainment experiences. People must have the time to peruse stores and malls, to frequent shops and to visit retail points. There must also be an almost inherent understanding of the process of entertainment. As well, shopping in this manner is considered to be the definitive modern statement. This manifests itself in a number of fascinating ways.

Leisure, in its early modern sense, already followed complex evolution. Although Aristotle had, centuries before, commented that leisure was "freedom from the necessity of labor," a great deal of what constitutes leisure today involves strenuous physical activity. For the ruling elites of the Middle Ages, leisure was oriented around training for war. Whether it was mock battles or hunting, actively moving around was a key component of what we would call leisure time. It is only at the end of the Middle Ages that more sedate past times become incorporated into the leisure format. Playing games such as chess and cards come into being on a significant scale at this time. As society became stabilized, more significant leisure activities became popular. These could include playing and listening to music and writing and reciting poetry. During the Renaissance, and in particular in northern Europe, as urban communities became more formalized, leisure pursuits originally associated with the elites spread to many more people. To some extent this had to do with the wealthy no longer being secluded away on manors and now living within the heart of urban environments. Consequently, their pastimes were more readily observed and more accessible to many more people.[1]

A very significant feature of this evolution had to do with the pursuit of fashion becoming a leisure activity. The elites, in their seeking out of amusements that reflected individual expression and in their desire for new and novel diversions, began to fixate on change or fashion. Gary Cross suggests that this spurred on the development of clothing industries and "stimulated the fur trade in North America." The quest for the latest and the newest became, in itself, a key form of leisure. Cross points out that this was quite removed from Aristotle's definition of leisure, but in a way, had more in common with what knights were doing. The obsession with fashion was reworked to become a gentler form of self-improvement that was complemented with etiquette and decorum.[2]

For the masses leisure was simply a break from the grueling regimen of work. Leisure could also take the form of a festival or a religious holiday in which games were played and food and drink were consumed. Activities could be unruly and get out of hand and many of the political, social, and increasingly religious elites sought to reign these in. Agriculture and its demands usually dictated the leisure calendar, especially in the pre-industrial period, and the vagaries of nature were also heavily influential in defining when it was time to work and when it was not. The notion of the Protestant work ethic greatly complicated matters, especially in northern Europe and also added a layer of disdain toward unstructured leisure pursuits. As society in Europe and, increasingly, the United States, moved to a more commercial foundation, the marketing of products that required leisure to consume greatly added to the acceptance of leisure time. Those who were selling things that revolved around "pleasure" became "the best propagandists for leisure."[3] This notion would be played out again and again throughout recent history.

As stores began to offer more goods they were open with greater frequency. In the bustling cities of Europe and North America, shops became key points in the fusing of leisure and entertainment. In order to accommodate as wide a clientele as possible, shopkeepers often stayed open until late at night. Shopping quickly became part of one's leisure experience because it often had pleasurable connotations. It was pleasant and enjoyable to talk to friends, to discuss the latest news, or to sip tea in a London bookshop. In the cramped and crowed apartments, which characterized many cities, going out to a shop was a liberating experience. This was especially pronounced as the Industrial Revolution took hold, radically changing the expectations of workers and craftsmen. A key to the change was the tangible division between leisure time and work time.[4]

As more money was being generated, more opportunities for leisure and entertainment arose. These included shorter workdays, free evenings, the weekend, and summer vacations.[5] What happened between the end of the nineteenth century and the beginning of the twentieth is that more people became accustomed to novelty as a form of entertainment and more had the time to indulge. The technology of the Crystal Palace and the railroad, of Thomas Cook's tours and dance halls, led to the wonders of the amusement park. Important as well was that these outlets were predicated on maximization of profits, which led to the creation of a mass entertainment industry. As Peter Stearns has recognized, the appeal of going to the department store to see and to look, in essence for "the experience," was a process almost identical to going to an amusement park, or later a film.[6]

By extension, as far as the comparison goes, a more direct correlation could be to the magnificent movie palaces, which were constructed in major cities during the 1910s and '20s. These were deliberate attempts to invest movies with an aura of glamour and they were quite successful. The architecture and the interior design of these palaces was all about the idea of transporting people away from the banal and the everyday, a superb complement to what was on the screen. Like the *Grand Magasins* they were all about fantasy and another world. David Nasaw cites a writer on this topic, one who suggests, "the palaces represented, indeed were, an alternative world, one richer, more romantic, and far more democratic than the mundane worlds the picture-palace customers inhabited on the outside."[7] For the average person entering into this luxury and finery, whether the department store or the movie palace, was a transforming experience.

Between the development of the first department stores in the 1850s and the first malls or shopping centers in the 1920s, numerous changes in the realms of transportation, communication, and technology greatly affected the opportunities to display and sell merchandise. Many of these phases were originally conceived for purposes other than consumption but in turn were reworked to alter and affect the shopping universe. From lighting to escalators, to synthetics and automobiles, inventions and developments in numerous areas came to have a significant impact on the availability, display, and purchase of goods. New building materials made it possible to create the vast emporiums of Paris, London, New York, and Chicago. New ideas in advertising, publicity and promotion, made the access factor a reality for many who previously would not have been able to partake in the shopping as an entertainment experience. All of these features coalesced around the "architectural drama" that surrounded the new urban department stores. As part of the "new urban monumentalism," these stores quickly challenged the traditional attractions of the cities and came to represent something supremely modern.[8]

In order to enhance the leisure and entertainment qualities of shopping it was important for two occurrences to have happened. One was the increasing conflation of "consumer goods" as primary objectives in the overall realm of culture. What this means is that it was vital to position these items as unique rather than a part of traditional facets of the cultural universe. This had the effect of bringing about their novelty and in turn encouraging a desire for them.[9] The second key feature—alluded to above —was the importance of utilizing technology and in particular electricity to facilitate and enhance shopping as entertainment experience. To some extent this came with the division of production and distribution, in the sense that consumption itself was increasingly thought of as "a social activity associated with leisure and entertainment." Consumers and shoppers in general came to equate shopping as an entertainment experience in due course because many of the great department stores were located very close to entertainment venues such as the theater.[10] Cities in the last part of the nineteenth century and early twentieth century had vibrant selections of amusements, which of course ran the gamut from the most lurid, to those on the high end of the culture spectrum.[11] Often what allowed for this flowering were technical developments.

Rosalynd Williams suggests that technology was employed to create endless possibilities in the retail realm. She suggests that technology "made possible the material realization of fantasies which had hitherto existed only in the realm of imagination." It was electricity or electrical power in particular that Williams feels was particularly important in allowing for a variety of results—especially the magic association with certain forms of entertainment consumption. "Electricity," she writes,

> created a fairy land environment, the sense of being, not in a distant place, but in a make-believe place where obedient genies leap to their master's command, where miracles of speed and motion are wrought by the slightest gesture, where a landscape of glowing pleasure domes and twinkling lights stretches into infinity.[12]

One way to delight and enthrall is to manipulate size and scale. From the miniature to the gigantic, extremes of area have always had the capacity to wow viewers and observers. In the case of the department stores, one of the most unique features of these emporiums was the size. Significant here, as was referred to in the introduction, is the fact that these institutions were compared to cathedrals. The purpose of the cathedral—at least the medieval one—was to inspire "awe."[13] The same process was at work and is still in place with department stores. This has been a staple of Western architecture for at least 1,000 years. Michael Miller recounts that the emphasis of bigness, largess, quantity and sheer hugeness, was a factor that was played up in the descriptions of the Parisian department stores. He writes that "everything about the store was 'immense,' 'vast,' 'gigantic,'" whether it was the basement or the gallery or the staircase.[14] Human beings seem naturally attracted to large and immense things; buildings and structures that are humongous in scope stagger the imagination. The department store, and later the mall, picked up on this.

For some the quaint shop or the little boutique work in the reverse manner. The attraction and charm of the confined space, when properly designed, has as much appeal in miniature as the vastness of the department store and mall.

This is utilized to the most successful degree at Disney World. On Main Street, the primary thoroughfare, the one which evokes the strongest associations with perceived nostalgic memories of small-town life, the buildings, many of which are shops, are smaller than actual size. The "five-eighths" rule is in effect here, a shrinkage that is not overt, but that is quite effective. These structures are smaller, five-eighths the size of traditional structures. Accordingly, "This scaling-down appeals psychologically to both children and adults; children find the smaller spaces more comfortable and comprehensible—more their size—while the adults . . . 'are reminded of trips back to childhood haunts; everything is much smaller than one remembers.'"[15]

In much of the critical literature that deals with popular culture, mass consumption and the built environment, the word "Disneyfication" has become synonymous with artifice and middlebrow expectation. There are commentators who appreciate some of the contributions that Disney culture has made but those are few and far between. In quite explicit terms, the ideals governing Disney World were deliberate attempts to transfer the magic of the movies onto a real landscape. Regardless of one's take on this seminal contributor to and influence upon the cultural landscape, much of what has occurred has been passed on or distilled into shopping as an entertainment experience. Whether one is discussing "Main Street," EPCOT or Celebration, the impact has been significant. Disney has been equated with entertainment and now has fully influenced shopping.[16]

This evolution has been markedly pronounced in the rise of the super malls, the WEM and the Mall of America being the dominant bookends of this trend. The success of the Disney formula was reconfigured at the Mall of America. While it was being constructed, Melvin Simon, one of the Mall of America's principal owners, stated that his environment was "going to be like going to Disneyland."[17] And it became so. In a deliberate, albeit modified way, the Mall of America mimicked Disney culture in the manner in which the entertainment experience merged with the shopping experience. There was a merging of the elements of the theme park with the large regional mall. What is salient to recognize is that "the mall industry looked to the Disney's enchanted kingdom, the flagship of the entertainment industry, for the re-enchantment of the consumer's experience at the mall."[18] The idea of re-enchantment is key, for that is a main factor in getting people into the mall and, importantly, getting the consumer to be receptive to the magic of the new mall environments. As with Disney culture and Disney "imagineering" specifically, the point is to "make the magic real." One could argue that perhaps the definitive aspect regarding the appeal of shopping as an entertainment experience is in fact translating elements of fantasy, luxury, and desire into concrete desire to purchase.[19] This process has a long history.

One of the most often-cited comparisons between shopping and entertainment has to do with the cinema. The movie-like similarities between stores and shopping and the best entertainment films are correlations that are often invoked. A related comparison comes up continuously in the form of theater and art.[20] The Department store—and historically, the "window"—and the current spate of museum-like boutiques are the most obvious examples of this. There was a defined "theatricality" to viewing the shopping store window and to going into the store. There is still a very theatrical element to most malls and to many stores. Designers are aware of how important it is to create the right ambience and to utilize the proper props. These act to invite the potential shopper in and to make him or her feel comfortable. The theatricality of certain retail environments, based on a combination of lighting, color, and overall arrangements, is enticing as well as comforting.[21]

This was taken to an extreme version by Simon Doonan at Barneys in New York during the late 1980s and 1990s. The downtown store became one of the most talked-about retail entities as a result of the creativity of the Pressman family and their in-house designer, Doonan. Originally charged with creating window displays, Doonan became the store's stylist and invented designs and tableaux dazzling in their originality. Almost every series of windows caught the attention of the press. People came downtown to see what all the buzz was about. New artists were encouraged to submit designs and works to accentuate the windows and generate even more notoriety. Barneys leaped ahead of its competition and became, both outside and inside, the most daring retail experiment. With its wild interiors, its famous parties, its startling windows, and new designers, it surpassed anything then in existence. Whenever a new season dawned, it came complete with a torrent of creativity and controversy that spilled out into the street and careened in all corners of New York. No longer was it simply a store, but it became an "event," a reason to go downtown, and later, a part of the itinerary to the Madison Avenue store. Barneys became a must see tourist destination. As Doonan writes, "The ambiance of the events was extrapolated into the day-to-day store ambiance and made a shopping excursion to Barneys feel totally different. Shopping at Barneys had become an event in itself, complete with celebrity attendees."[22]

In harmony with late nineteenth-century and early twentieth-century developments, the visual nature of shopping took on a more defined role. One of the dominant communication technologies that have facilitated consumption in an entertainment version has been the development of the cinema. As Anne Friedberg has stated,

> Movie-going was analogous to browsing without the obligation to buy. The cinema spectator engaged in the contemplative visual examination of lifestyles and products, of characters and behaviors, imaginatively 'tried on' other identities.[23]

Friedberg relates that for virtually nothing, the average person could peruse the department store and take part in this visual spectacle. Learning to see in this new environment required some lessons and some time, but it was easy to do and enthralling to partake in once one became accustomed to looking in this world of stimulation. To some extent it grew to be fun and entertaining—as it still is. But one had to learn to see in a new way. In his often-cited text on the nature and structure of the retail store, William Green writes: "The importance of store image is best exemplified by comparing a store to a movie."[24] Accordingly, Green implies, when someone goes to see a film, there are certain expectations that must be fulfilled. The same process is at work with a store. Expectations derived from visual signs, lighting, material use, music, and a host of other features must be met. A form of this could be the "commodified gaze."[25]

When things—material possessions, of almost any kind, are recontextualized they often take on both a brand new set of qualities and also a new image. A motorcycle is a transportation commodity that has certain components. On the street or in the showroom it is one thing; in the Guggenheim museum it is reconfigured as art. Placing a dazzling array of products in a specially created atmosphere has the effect of making these products more appealing to many people. We become attracted to things that are grouped or positioned in an aesthetically appealing way. Part of this comes from the importance of display, which has been accentuated by lighting, color and position. In an art gallery, according to Peter Corrigan, this has the effect of "exciting the senses." The same occurs within the confines of the department store: "the most mundane of objects becomes desirable through display."[26] Corrigan implies that something special occurs, a magical-process-involving spectacle seems to kick in at this point.

This declares itself in a number of ways. The lusciousness and quantity become overwhelming to the average shopper. The use of lighting and, increasingly, smell, seem to glorify the mundane. One of the reasons why perfume counters are often placed at the front or entrance to many stores is the key impact of smell. The same goes for why perfume and cologne testers approach the shopper as soon as she or he comes in. Smell is a significant pathway to emotion and plays both a conscious and unconscious role in provoking a consumer. According to the author of an authoritative textbook on store design, "people who smell something may be emotionally affected, even though they may not even be aware of the smell. This makes the use of odors to create emotional effects a potentially powerful tool."[27]

Charging the merchandise with a special set of associations, or "exciting meanings" by contextualizing them, also adds to the atmosphere. As with Bloomingdale's and its focus on particular places to promote specific goods, Corrigan writes that

> it was also common to infuse objects with the exciting meanings of exotic places, and this was accomplished by presenting them against a background that spoke of, say, the Orient—a department store might be transformed into an Egyptian temple or a Japanese garden . . . Exotically charged objects are probably among the most desirable of all, and the department stores went to elaborate lengths to stage objects in a way that promised exotic experiences.[28]

As travel agencies and tourist organizations well know, converting a basic place or beach into something exotic has great appeal to prospective holiday seekers. Many associations seem to surface when a place or thing is subverted from the mundane into the exotic. The perception, which is key, provides a potential experience that captivates and in turn sells. And this is by no means a new phenomenon. The early department stores regularly stated extravagant shows designed to offer up the most unique merchandise from "exotic" locales, whether Turkish or Egyptian. These often came complete with performers and music. In London, Liberty's and Selfridge's both took on the role as commercial foreign affairs correspondents. Through these stores, people gleaned popular knowledge about "oriental" societies. These of course were often accentuated through the use of fantastic photographs that served, for many, as their first glimpse of these exotic destinations.[29] One can convincingly argue that this form of exoticism is enormously appealing to shoppers seeking an entertainment experience.

Las Vegas has been reinvented as a tourist-shopping destination. The plethora of new hotels that bring the world to Las Vegas comes hand in hand with shopping as an entertainment experience.[30] The Venetian Hotel complex is a full recreation of Venice, complete with canals and major historical sites, painstakingly recreated in Las Vegas. The shopping element is right up front. At the heart of the complex is the massive Grand Canal Shoppes, where, according to the official brochure, "Shoppers will be transported to another time and place in a festival-like atmosphere, including serenading gondoliers, artisans, glass blowers and masque makers."[31] The ability to shop, in the most fantastic of atmospheres is a key part of the attraction and, increasingly, a key component in visiting the city.

Desert Passage in Las Vegas, adjacent to the Aladdin Resort and Casino takes the shopping as entertainment experience to a completely new level. This unabashed "shopping adventure" utilizes the associations of exotica and marketing by merging the architecture of India and Morocco to create a modern bazaar. One would think that one was on the streets of Fez, given all the attention to detail. From dancers and acrobats, to pedicabs to security guards outfitted in costumes, the atmosphere is overwhelming. With its *trompe l'oeil* ceilings, evoking an azure sky, to its outdoor markets, its "Lost City," reminiscent of Petra, it moves to a more extreme recreation than the Venetian. Like the most exquisitely detailed movie sets, the Desert Passage has fabrications that are literally mind-boggling. Over 100 different plaster finishes were employed and "painted finishes were 'aged'" to give the effect of oil tarnish. Researchers went out to Morocco and consulted with agents of the Moroccan government to find the best ideas and locate the best craftsmen. Tenants, selected for a variety of factors that were harmonious with the structure's aura, are like actors on a movie set, who are motivated to perform in a very specific way. Desert Passage has moved the entertainment experience of shopping to a very sophisticated level. By utilizing architecture, acting, and themes a "narrative" is created. Environment has become a significant aspect in this evolution.[32]

If the cinema and the movie are utilized in numerous ways, so too must the enormous influence of television. In the merging of theater, film, the stage, and design, it has been television that has perhaps had the most important influence on shopping as an entertainment experience. William Kowinski pondered this relationship nearly twenty years ago. He asked, how do so many surrender so willingly to the artificial atmosphere created by retail firms? When he posed this question, the e-store was in its infancy and the sophisticated environments created by Niketown and other outlets were not yet a factor in the retail landscape. In his pioneering work on mall culture and the universe created by these structures, he wondered, "How can this [artificial mall culture] be such a powerful and attractive fantasy that it compensates for what's missing—like the sky, or a little bit of fleshly disorder? How can people accept roofed-over trees, patently artificial effects, and outdoor cafes that aren't really outdoors?"[33]

In searching for an answer, he found a journalist who suggested that the acceptance of the above comes from television's ability to manage people's "perceptions of space and reality" and to persuade people to suspend their disbelief." Kowinski suggests that because the mall environment, like the department store environment, is such a visual one, the images on television are transferred to the visual nature of the mall. Whether it is about familiarity or televisual acceptance, does not matter. The inconsistencies and incongruities of retail environments are processed through the eye of someone who is quite comfortable changing channels on a continuous basis.[34] This last point is rather nicely illustrated in the film *Scenes from a Mall*, starring Woody Allen and Bette Midler. The two characters portrayed by Allen and Midler roam a mall and interact with stores and products as part of the structure of the film. They buy themselves trinkets and gifts, which give them ephemeral delight in much the same way that watching television acts as a temporary pleasure point. The enormous variety of goods and the constantly changing design and display of merchandise and stores, respectively, is also characteristic of television, and significantly, of channel surfing.[35]

If film and television are considered important, if not vital contributors to the acceptance of shopping as an entertainment experience, the employment of music and all its peripherals must also be factored in. No longer is the staid Muzak of the past employed. Either there is a loud booming sound, similar to that found in a dance club, complete with monitors showing videos or else more subtle forms of music are employed. These run the gamut from classical music found in more upscale venues to new age accompaniment found in nature and science stores. Many chains employ music consultants and some individual stores have in-house DJ's playing music. At Armani Exchange, the president of the chain reiterates the importance of music to the image of the store and to the shopping experience:

> Music is the most important part of our language. Youth and music go together. Any chance we get to bring music to the brand experience is success for us. We've updated our store sound systems, so the A/X customer feels very at home. We play dance music, and an A/X version of rap, all music very specific to our demographic. We're bringing out our fourth CD, Chemistry, for [the] holiday. And we're launching a CD gift set.[36]

When stores start to produce their own CDs, which often promote with the image they wish to project of the synergy between shopping and entertainment, the relationship has become even tighter. The success of the Starbucks CDs is another example of this aural merging of shopping as an entertainment experience.

In a series of questions put to a middle-aged gentleman that focused on leisure activities and shopping preferences engaged in on the weekend, the respondent replied that he takes his two sons to car dealerships as an activity at least once a month. Car dealerships, he wrote, provide an outlet for him and his sons to look at new models, to test-drive vehicles and to explore and experience the automotive culture that he and his sons find so stimulating. From Japan to Germany, car manufacturers are increasingly aware of this component in the process and have reacted accordingly. They have taken the elements of the theme park and merged them with aspects of entertainment culture to create a supreme entertainment experience. Near Wolfsburg, the home of Volkswagen, there is a huge theme park "devoted to the four-wheeled object of desire." According to Otto Riewoldt, "each of the Group's brands has its own pavilion in what is tantamount to a polytheistic place of worship, dotted with temples dedicated to the gods of the brands."[37] There are many such structures all over the world. People make pilgrimages to places like Atlanta, Georgia, or Hershey, Pennsylvania, to see how their favorite consumer goods are made and constructed, what their history is, and how they have been marketed over time.

One of the appealing features of the above scene is the ability for consumers to touch and be a part of the retail environment. It has been recognized that one of the most pleasing satisfactions is allowance for a tactile relationship with a product and even a service. Unlike in a traditional museum environment (although interactivity is increasingly available in museums) an enormous amount of good will, excitement, and satisfaction is built up and exchanged when people can touch, handle, try, or taste the product. In the upscale grocery stores as well as in the big box outlets, allowing the customers to engage in a taste of some new product is a mutually successful arrangement. With endless quantities of sampling going on in these stores, it is not uncommon for people to almost 'eat dinner' on the free food offerings available. That, for some, is truly novel.

Despite the fact that society is oriented increasingly around high performance and a mediated world, the satisfactions gained for the simple, yet potent act of touching, handling, or caressing the merchandise are huge. Stand in any store and watch how many people run their fingers over the coats and shirts, the shiny kitchen appliance or the sleek electronic good. Paco Underhill feels that this is the reason why so many companies give away samples. These free selections do wonders to establish an exciting bond.[38] This is especially pronounced when consumers are given the opportunity to taste or try something that they have seen on television advertising.

At the other end of this spectrum is what one could term, "nostalgic entertainment." Whether utilizing the soda-fountain appeal of a mythical

1950s creation or attempting to harness the pleasantness and security of a 1970s basement, not to mention the potency of a "main street" set, many developers, stores, and retail designers have picked up on the grand appeal of nostalgia as a theme in shopping as an entertainment experience. This comes in the elaborate and exacting reproductions found in many stores and restaurants, as it does in the settings chosen. From Old Navy's use of settings that suggest a cross between a market and a small town general store, to the elaborate props accenting a men's store, the effect is enticing. And, regardless if it inspires comfort or longing, it certainly is entertaining. This marketing trend is inherently appealing to baby-boomers and those moving towards middle age.[39] When a positive and "authentic" re-creation of the past is successful, it is intensely attractive to potential consumers. Whether translated through props, design, environment, or products, it becomes to many an almost tangible touchstone to the past. This "verisimilitude—the illusion of reality conveyed by faithfully depicted details," trigger a form of empathy akin to the way viewers feel when watching a film with sympathetic performers. The audience gets into or sincerely "feels into" a "person, object, or activity" that has been portrayed.[40] This explains the powerful connection between consumers and certain products as well as between shoppers and certain stores. The constructed worlds of Ralph Lauren have been enormously successful at harnessing this often-intangible state of mind.

Retailers, mall-development corporations, and many others have come to the conclusion that utilizing the products of mass entertainment to bring shoppers into shopping centers and malls is a significant way to increase interest. It is, to some extent, increasingly what customers expect. According to one prominent architect who addressed the International Council of Shopping Centers, "Entertainment is part of the future of the shopping center." Patrick Brege, who has designed sets and theatres for Cirque du Soleil is well situated to make such an assessment. He justifies the cost by saying the highly entertaining environments bring in the customers.[41] The emphasis on the entertainment focus is something that is being applied to malls across North America in order to give them new life. Malls that have been around since the 1970s have undergone major facelifts and renovations. If there are not overt entertainment elements, then a host of subtle aspects have been employed in order to stimulate more interest. Many of these fall into the category of entertainment features. These subtle changes make the mall or the store more exciting and more appealing. Another aspect of this is to reinvigorate shopping in general and to once again, make it appealing.

This is the attempt to make shopping an amusement. As one developer put it, "the fun of shopping went away—we're trying to bring the fun of shopping back."[42] This idea is particularly resonant with regard to the growth of big box power centers. A significant difference here is that these developments are outside and are anchored by large stores. People come to visit one or two stores and then leave. In order to keep them around, developers such as Sterling Centrecorp are constructing multipurpose "life-style" centers, which include hotels, entertainment centers, hockey rinks, bars, as well as stores.[43]

The stimulation of the shopping environment has always contained entertainment qualities. What has occurred is that after a time, what was at one time satisfying and entertaining becomes stale. Simply gazing at a store window is not as likely to stimulate or enthrall in the same manner as it once did. Clowns and dancers can only appeal for so long. And, given the fact that so many other entertainment venues have jaded consumers in their expectations, the move is on to find new ways to enrapture and enchant shoppers. Consequently, the bounds of entertainment in the shopping realm have been flung open. Whether it is Camp Snoopy at The Mall of America or the wave pool at the West Edmonton Mall, the boundaries have been elongated. According to Ann Satterthwaite, "the scale and sophistication of these entertainments differ considerably from the entertainments traditionally associated with shopping."[44]

As society moves toward a stronger emphasis on visual spectacle, shopping environments have kept pace and in a number of instances, have been at the forefront of this postmodern process. When discussing the concept of spectacle, most theorists invoke Guy Debord's 1960s text, *The Society of the Spectacle*, a work, that is hyper-critical of mass consumer culture. More subdued and less personal interpretations of spectacle point to different conclusions. Spectacle, as defined by a variety of theorists, means an interaction of deep ocular icons in an intensive setting that engage and enthrall. Modern culture is particularly rich in these offerings, and shopping environments have risen to the fore as examples of spectacle. What is unique as far as shopping as an entertainment experience is the fact that the consumer is aware of and often willing to participate in the experience of spectacle.[45]

What has been achieved has been the creation of an otherworldly experience. This liminal reaction is significant and perhaps definitive in making shopping an entertaining experience. It is the feeling or the intense array of feelings that we seek out and desire in the world of consumption. Like Disneyland, the conscious attempt is to shuffle the senses to a level that is extraordinarily pleasing. This is the magical sensation that people receive: they are excited, overwhelmed, calmed, focused, dreamy—all at the same time. Rightly or wrongly, morally appropriate or sinister in its calculation, shopping is so pleasing and so enticing because it transports people away from their mundane existences. The bells and whistles, the impressive displays, the wonderful attractions all combine to create this power in a way that virtually no other force in western society is capable of paralleling.

George Ritzer defines "spectacle" as a "dramatic public display." This can exist as intentional creations, which he calls "extravaganzas," or as unintentional process.[46] Ritzer is concerned that the process of spectacular consumption within environments that are essentially retail stores has permeated society as a whole. There is a constant pressure to become more and more spectacular and to literally seek to engage the entertainment customer with more and more spectacle. Part of the reason for this ongoing focus has been the retailers themselves. Shopping had to be exciting and spectacular; it had to become an entertainment process.[47] Yet, the marketplaces, be it the agora, arcade, or atrium, always offered something different. It was always unique in that it was exciting and dynamic, social, and active. What was available there to see or to touch, to buy or to smell, was a spectacle in itself. To some extent, what happened during the nineteenth century was an unheard-of situation, but to a significant extent, it was something that the original department store visionaries knew from the start.

NOTES

1. Gary Cross, *A Social History of Leisure Since 1600* (State College, Penn.: Venture Publishing, 1990), 16–17.

2. Cross, *A Social History of Leisure Since 1600*, 17.

3. Cross, *A Social History of Leisure Since 1600*, 19–27, 36.

4. Cross, *A Social History of Leisure Since 1600*, 48, 62.

5. Cross, *A Social History of Leisure Since 1600*, 73.

6. Cross, *A Social History of Leisure Since 1600*, 123, and Peter N. Stearns, *Consumerism in World History: The Global Transformation of Desire* (London: Routlege, 2001), 44–49.

7. David Nasaw, *Going Out: The Rise and Fall of Public Amusements* (Cambridge, Mass.: Harvard University Press, 2002), 239.

8. Geoffrey Crossick and Serge Jaumain, "The World of the Department Store: Distribution, Culture and Social Exchange," in *Cathedrals of Consumption: The European Department Store, 1850–1939*, eds. Geoffrey Crossick and Serge Jaumain (Aldershot: Ashgate, 1999), 21.

9. Rosalynd Williams, *Dream Worlds: Mass Consumption in Late Nineteenth-Century France* (Berkeley: University of California Press, 1986), excerpt in David Crowley and Paul Heyer, *Communication in History*, third edition (New York: Longman, 1999) 166.

10. Crossick and Jaumain, "The World of the Department Store," 23.

11. See Nasaw, *Going Out*, 1–18.

12. Williams, *Dream Worlds*, 167.

13. Jackson Spielvogel, *Western Civilization* (New York: Thomson/Nelson, 2003) and William Chester Jordan, *Europe In the High Middle Ages* (New York: Viking/Penguin, 2003).

14. Michael Miller, *The Bon Marche: Bourgeois Culture and the Department Store, 1869–1920* (Princeton, N.J.: Princeton University Press, 1981), 174.

15. Cited in William Severini Kowinski, *The Malling of America: An Inside Look at the Great Consumer Paradise* (New York: William Morrow and Company, 1985), 67.

16. See Tom Vanerbilt, "It's a Mall World After All," *Harvard Design Magazine*, no. 9 (Fall 1999).

17. Cited in Gabian Faurholt Csaba and Soren Askegaard, "Malls and the Orchestration of the Shopping Experience in a Historical Perspective," *Advances in Consumer Research* vol. 26 (College Park: Association for Consumer Research, 1999), 38.

18. Csaba and Askegaard, "Malls and the Orchestration of the Shopping Experience in a Historical Perspective," 38.

19. Csaba and Askegaard, "Malls and the Orchestration of the Shopping Experience in a Historical Perspective," 38.

20. Erika Diane Rappaport, *Shopping For Pleasure: Women In the Making of London's West End* (Princeton, N.J.: Princeton University Press, 2000), 178.

21. James J. Farrell, *One Nation Under Goods: Malls and the Seductions of American Shopping* (Washington, D.C.: Smithsonian, 2003), 54–56.

22. Simon Doonan, *Confessions of a Window Dresser* (New York: Viking/Callaway, 1998), 115.

23. Anne Friedberg, ". . . 'therefore I am': The Shopper-Spectator and Transubstantiation through Purchase," in *Shopping: A Century of Art and Consumer Culture*, eds. Christoph Grunenberg and Max Hollein (Frankfurt: Hatje Cantz Publishers, 2002), 63.

24. William Green, *The Retail Store: Design and Construction* (San Jose: iUniverse.com, Inc., 2001), 1.

25. Anne Friedberg, ". . .'therefore I am': The Shopper-Spectator and Transubstantiation through Purchase," 65.

26. Peter Corrigan, *The Sociology of Consumption: An Introduction* (London: SAGE Publications, 1997), 57.

27. Green, *The Retail Store*, 12. Green writes: "There are two ways of influencing shoppers with fragrances, conspicuous and subliminal. Conspicuous odors have been used for many years as a form of olfactory merchandising. The intent is to use a recognizable smell to evoke a pleasant emotional sensation or memory in the customers. Many of these recalled memories are of childhood experiences, such as the smell of coffee brewing in the morning or bread or pies baking in the oven. . . . Conspicuous smells cause people to relax, and so their use in stores can evoke a particular image or mood. For example, a store selling swimwear may introduce the smell of coconut oil; a candy store may use cotton candy; and a lingerie shop may employ a potpourri fragrance. . . ."

28. Peter Corrigan, *The Sociology of Consumption*, 58.

29. See Mica Nava, "Women, the City and the Department Store," in *The Shopping Experience*, eds. Pasi Falk and Colin Campbell (London: SAGE Publications, 1997), 67.

30. See Giovanna Franci, *Dreaming of Italy: Las Vegas and the Virtual Grand Tour*, photographs by Federico Zignani (Reno: University of Nevada Press, 2005).

31. Cited in James B. Twitchell, *Living It Up: Our Love Affair With Luxury* (New York: Columbia University Press, 2002), 248.

32. Michael D. Beyard, et. al., *Developing Retail Entertainment Destinations*, Second Edition (Washington, D. C.: Urban Land Institute, 2001), 160–167.

33. Kowinski, *The Malling of America*, 71.

34. Kowinski, *The Malling of America*, 71.

35. Russel W. Belk and Wendy Bryce, "Christmas Shopping Scenes," *International Journal of Research in Marketing* 10 (1993), 283.

36. Sandra O'Loughlin, "A/X Armani Exchange Designs Hip Message," *Brandweek* 45, no. 42 (November 22, 2004), 9.

37. Otto Riewoldt, "Brandscaping," in *Brandscaping: Worlds of Experience in Retail Design*, edited by Otto Riewoldt (Berlin: Birkhauser Publishers, 2002), 9.

38. Paco Underhill, *Why We Buy: The Science of Shopping* (New York: Simon & Schuster, 1999), 162.

39. Barbara B. Stern, "Historical and Personal Nostalgia in Advertising Text: The *Fin de siecle* Effect," *Journal of Advertising* 21, no. 4 (December 1992), 12–13.

40. Stern, "Historical and Personal Nostalgia in Advertising Text," 16.

41. Albert Warson, "Mall Magic," *Building* 53, no. 6 (December 2003/January 2004), 15, 16.

42. Cited in Peter Brieger, "Life-style Shopping Arrives," *The National Post* (October 3, 2003), FP 3.

43. Peter Brieger, "Life-style Shopping Arrives," *The National Post* (October 3, 2003), FP 3.

44. Ann Satterthwaite, *Going Shopping: Consumer Choices and Community Consequences* (New Haven/London: Yale University Press, 2001), 229.

45. See Guy Debord, *The Society of the Spectacle* (New York: Zone Books, 1995), Jean Baudrillard, *Simulacra and Simulations* (New York: Semiotes(E), 1983), and A. Fuat Firat and Alladi Venkatesh, "Liberatory Postmodernism and the Reenchantment of Consumption," *Journal of Consumer Research* 22, no. 3 (December 1995), 239–267.

46. George Ritzer, *Enchanting a Disenchanted World*, Second Edition (Thousand Oaks, Calif.: Pine Forge/Sage, 2005), 93.

47. George Ritzer, *Enchanting a Disenchanted World*, 100.

3

+

The Department Store

In the United States prior to the coming of the department store, people depended on dry goods firms and wholesalers to purchase goods.[1] Consequently, one could argue that the idea of shopping as defined by Anne Friedberg did not exist until the arrival of the department store. The distinguishing feature in this context was, that entering a shop "entailed an obligation to make a purchase."[2] Within the department store, potential customers were, historically, encouraged to browse, and prompted to take their time and peruse the vast array of goods and services. There was no pressure to spend money in these new emporiums; people could come and literally be enthralled by what they saw. In Britain, Paris, and selected cities within the United States it was possible to walk through the aisles of these new emporiums and gaze around at what was available. One could "dream" without necessarily buying. This ability, to wander and browse, was revolutionary in the sense that according to Bill Lancaster, it offered a totally "new type of liberty."[3] As well, this lack of pressure—this freedom—constitutes half of the leisure equation. The other half came from the fact that it was something to do for the day. Women could "do the town" for the day and sample everything that the new department stores had to offer. It could become a hobby; just walking through was entertainment enough.[4]

These new environments quickly became and to a great extent still are[5] "places where consumers are an audience to be entertained by commodities, where selling is mingled with amusement, where arousal of free floating desire is as important as immediate purchase of particular items."[6] By the early decades of the twentieth century, shopping had matured from the

31

prosaic buying. It had become, thanks to a number of innovations, much more involved than simply looking and selecting. The fantastic shopping emporiums brought in people from all walks of life and literally enthralled them with both the content and the surroundings. As well, shopping had evolved into a "total experience in which the retailer became a subtle advisor on personal taste."[7] This was a seminal development in itself, for it brought people—and in particular women—into the stores and allowed them the time to peruse, select, sample and, importantly, to socialize. During the late Victorian and Edwardian periods, London's West End had an air of glamour and delight and became a central zone where shopping and entertainment coalesced, especially for women.[8]

The female shopper, or the female consumer, was a key attribute in the reorientation of shopping as an entertainment focus. On the one hand, in the eighteenth century, it was predominantly aristocratic women or, at the other extreme, those far from virtuous who patronized shops as a diversionary activity that met the entertainment elements, but this audience began to change as shopping became more modern and thus more acceptable. As shops evolved into boutiques and eventually, nascent department store emporiums, it became common for middle-class women to patronize these establishments. Here, the use of technology becomes important in accentuating the entertainment features. Lighting made shopping safer and more visible. Counter space, mirrors, and a variety of other developments opened up the store in numerous ways that in turn made shopping less of a suspect activity.[9] This process would only be enhanced by innovations such as plate glass, air conditioning, elevators, and escalators in later decades. In turn, these changes reoriented the entertainment aspect of shopping. Although, many central elements remained unchanged.

Shopping, especially at fashionable shops and the new, glamorous department stores, was for women both liberating and at the same time restricting. Once one got caught up in the vagaries of the shopping expedition, one could run the risk of becoming a slave to fashion and material culture. As Rachel Bowlby writes,

> the shop that perpetually incites its customers to want ever more things can be seen as a form of psychological imprisonment: the *irresistible* object exerts a force as much as it elicits a longing. The metaphor of incarceration gains force from the circumstances that department stores did indeed form an enclosed, self-contained environment, with everything under one roof.[10]

The antidote to this could be found in the *flaneur* and the female equivalent, the *flaneuse*. The sense of freedom from confinement that an individual could receive from walking the streets in search of shopping as entertainment could be quite liberating. Women, in the modern period, did not have to be shut up in the home. They could indulge in the autonomy that the shopping street or department store had to offer.[11]

To some extent this process is still ongoing. In the east, the streets of Shanghai, for example, are extremely crowded with people walking around and looking at shops and stores. People leave their small apartments and seek an outlet in window and stall shopping that is a very key form of entertainment.

Sophisticated retail environments have never been content to simply let the goods lie on the table or on the rack. Very quickly it was realized that to differentiate from the bazaar or boutique, what one had to do was entice the potential consumer, educate and offer more than the basic staples of goods and the mundane chore of buying. The early French department store magnates began, almost immediately, to offer a wide array of extra-consumption activities, which ranged from elaborate window displays to hair dressing salons. These entrepreneurs knew that they had to come up with something fantastic to entrance and attract the crowds. It was, as Michael Miller has observed, about "seduction and showmanship."[12] The founder of the Bon Marché, Aristide Boucicaut, was at the forefront in the game of dazzling potential consumers. He had the unparalleled ability to envelope

> his marketplace in an aura of fascination that turned buying into a special and irresistible occasion. Dazzling and sensuous, the Bon Marché became a permanent fair, an institution, a fantasy world, a spectacle of extraordinary proportions, so that going to the store became an event and an adventure. One came now less to purchase a particular article than simply to visit, buying in the process because it was part of the excitement, part of the experience that added another dimension to life.[13]

These offerings captivated the public who came to both expect and see the department store as a place filled with novelty. By the end of the nineteenth century, consumers flocked to the department store to be entertained and enthralled as much as to purchase. To some, the department store became a theater, to others, a temple. Both within, and increasingly on the outside, the department store was capable of resembling both.[14]

Harrods, the Knightsbridge landmark, has always been a major player in the desire to entertain its shoppers. Whether visiting its grand food halls or walking through its toy department, it is one of the most famous department stores in the world and a must-see tourist destination when visiting London. According to the store's official history, Harrods has always offered a variety of entertainments to its customers. What differentiates Harrods the store has often been the quality and the understated elegance with which these spectacles have been performed.

Like its American and French counterparts, the store had traditional shopping-as-entertainment-experience offerings, such as the restaurant and the tea garden, which became a primary "social rendezvous" in the early part of the century. It had clubs for men and women and was associated with the rich and famous. Its branding was pioneering; the green and gold bags and the lettering are pervasive throughout the world. Little by little the store became a seminal feature on the London tour, for both tourists and day visitors. In the late thirties, Harrods commissioned famous artists to design their ceramics and their art gallery and the book, manuscript and map room also appealed to high culture consumers. But Harrods environment differed from full scale shopping spectacle. It was sedate and cultured, structured around having an almost BBC-like mission to wean the population upward. An example of this was having children's author Enid Blyton read to children in the book department.[15]

Whereas women were the prime targets for department stores, men were also sought out as customers and clients. One of the issues was the association of the department store as a feminine zone and thus, stores such as Harrods attempted to lure the male consumer by positioning areas of this retail area in masculine terms. From smoking rooms to club-like lounges, offers of a shave, and reading rooms where newspapers and magazines were available, retailers like Harrods and Whiteley's attempted to entice the male consumer.[16]

The American department store magnate, John Wanamaker's store in Philadelphia, became one of the most appealing emporiums, to native city dwellers as well as to tourists. Wanamaker, who at first offered space to the city's other merchants in order to create a nascent mall, opened dozens of stores within a large space that literally rivaled what could be seen at the Philadelphia Centennial Exposition of 1876. Key to his success was his talent as a "showman."[17] At Wanamaker's there was a never-ending array of spectacles. According to Leon Harris, there was:

"theater, diversion, relaxation, education, celebration, a never-ending indoor fair full of hoopla, novelty, variety, performance, drama, sensationalism and *fun.*" Wannamaker utilized the above to an extent that had never before been seen. One of the first radio broadcasts came from the roof of his store in his New York City location.[18]

In London this idea of theatricality and excitement was also utilized by Gordon Selfridge. Gordon Selfridge had been Chicago department store magnate Marshall Fields's right hand man. He perfected the shopping-as-an-entertainment-experience ethos and transferred and improved upon it in London. Selfridge's department store was deliberately designed to "strike awe in the hearts of Londoners." More to the point, Selfridge consciously set out to wow his audience of prospective consumers by equating an aura of theatricality around the store. From its highly publicized opening to the impressive displays in the windows, the notion of theater was part and parcel of the store on a constant basis.[19]

Like the Bon Marché in Paris, Selfridge's was oriented around amusement and spectacle as much, if not more so, than mere commerce. Utilizing the latest advertising and public relations tactics, Selfridge's taught shoppers that visiting this store was a full-fledged experience in leisure time and not some mundane act of labor. The store itself was created as an antidote to the dark and dank and cluttered emporiums and was re-created as an almost heavenly, ethereal counterpoint to what had been in place previously. Going to the store became a truly "delightful pastime."[20] According to Erika Rappaport, the advertising strategy behind Selfridge's was deliberately structured to equate shopping with a leisure activity. Selfridge's attempted to convince women that the store would provide them with a stimulating series of social activities that blended the best of mass and elite culture. Rappaport describes the content of the advertisement as being filled with comparisons to carnivals, fairs, and festivals.[21] Selfridge's pioneered another variation in the realm of the department store as theater. Demonstrations of virtually every kind would occur in the store. These ranged from introducing new kinds of electrical products to gymnastics displays.[22]

The idea of a store being a form of public theater was something that was taken quite seriously. The burgeoning industries that grew up accommodating the department store acknowledged that the theatrical element within the store put "shoppers in the mood to consume." The fact that windows involved highly sophisticated arrangements of lighting and stage design, and that fashion shows and other forms of entertainment all became strategic touch stones in the display process illustrates the degree of seriousness with which this was all taken.[23] The theatrical motif dominated, yet it was not the only leisure-inspired mechanism employed.

Simply entering the store was a wonderful experience for many people. It was so large and grand, so tall and big, that they willingly got lost. Wandering through the displays and the maze-like constructions of merchandise provided a thrill for many early customers. One never knew where one would end up or what one could see. In many early department stores, there was a huge skylight, often made of stained glass. They could walk to the center and look up.[24]

The American Marshall Fields was a pioneer as well in the move to make the department store as stimulating as possible to the would-be buyer. Fields's was instrumental in turning the department store into a museum-like atmosphere, which offered the consumer something *more*. This 'something more' turned the traditional notion of a retail emporium completely on its head. Consumers, and in particular women, could not just shop, but they could enjoy tea, indulge in a manicure, and even watch a fashion show. All these subsidiary activities could be undertaken within the confines of Fields's palace. These distractions and novelties, transformed a day, an afternoon, or even an evening, into an entertainment experience.[25]

The list of entertainment and leisure activities available at the new department stores seemed to expand and broaden on a constant basis. Aristide Boucicaut's Bon Marché had a reading room, an art gallery, and was the site of many concerts, which would attract thousands.[26] At Siegel Coopers in New York City, one could purchase not only a myriad of staples but view the world's largest photographic gallery and peruse one of the most enormous petstores anywhere—complete with lions and tropical birds.[27] One could now be enthralled and entertained at the department store in the same manner that previously could be had by taking in a gallery or going to the zoo. Going to a department store now meant going out.

Theater was a significant draw in most any manifestation. The fashion show, which originated in the United States around 1907, became a major entertainment event in the constellation of offerings at most major stores and at times was capable of drawing thousands of spectator consumers. The newly discovered modern activity of window shopping enticed people to come and look but also to be entertained by the highly innovative and creative windows designed by some of the most artistic people that could be found. Store windows in themselves became hugely popular attractions and were, in some cases, elevated to art forms. The work of Frank L. Baum, future author of the *Wizard of Oz*, created scenes of unparalleled creativity. In some cities, the windows were covered on Sundays, out of respect for the Lord's Day, which made Monday a particularly anticipated day. The glass window also allowed for the shopper or the viewer to see their own reflection while at the same time serving as a visible barrier between viewer and content, all the while heightening the level of desirability. Music in the form of orchestras, bands, and trios playing in various places throughout the stores provided acoustic accompaniment and a mood enhancing feeling. Dining was a novel way to bring the consumer in and to keep them there. Stores featured a wide array of culinary options, which ranged from extreme fine dining to quick meals and tea service.[28]

Beyond music, one of the more unique ways to entice consumers to the store was to offer elements of culture that were commonly associated with the museum or the gallery. The department store came about at the same time as the birth of the modern museum and thus, it possessed many of the same attributes of the museum. According to Neil Harris, "like museums, department stores were selective concentrations of merchandise,

merchandise grouped by functional categories rather than by age and nationality."[29] Many department stores began to take on a museum-like atmosphere, complete with "dark wood cases" and in some areas "cluttered interiors."[30] Art exhibits were quite common, as were 'themed' rooms, both of which borrowed heavily from the conventions of the art gallery and the history museum. Department stores were often the first place that patrons saw both modern and American art. After viewing the Armory show of 1913, the Gimbel brothers became "among the most ardent supporters of modern art, buying up Cezanne's, Picasso's, and Braques', and displaying them in the store galleries in Cincinnati, New York, Cleveland, and Philadelphia."[31] The art, the decor, the general international flavor of the stores reflected the fact that they were now competing with museums and virtually every other existant entertainment offering. Department stores came to be seen as micro worlds, fairs, places where one could go and sample material history, food, fashion, and culture from all over the world.[32]

As a surrogate for the art gallery, museum, fair, carnival, theater, music hall, and restaurant, the department store became the repository of entertainment needs for many members of the urban middle and upper-middle class. Just as today, the museum/gallery gift store is the inversion of this equation (see chapter 7); the department store offered those who entered through its doors the chance to experience a variety of entertainment offerings.

The appeal of luxury, presented in often unheard of ways, was a significant entertainment draw for many people, especially women. Many department stores surround their environs with wood and chandeliers, fabrics and all the vestiges of the better classes. Tearooms were common, complete with silver and rich linen, and fancy restaurants also bespoke of a world only temporarily accessible. In many cases this was in counterpoint to the small quarters and mundane surroundings in which many lived.[33]

Luxury and entertainment, enthrallment and liminality could also be stimulated and created by the abundance of goods on display. Walking into the store and being overwhelmed by the quantity of goods available, the variety of textures, the multiplicity of colors, the selection of different things and their overall display, could certainly enchant the average consumer in a manner equal to seeing a film. Increasingly, as consumption defines people in the West, this captivating capacity of selection remains appealing. This is significant in a number of respects.

Rachel Bowlby implies that there is a severe difference between shopping at the department store and the supermarket. She writes,

Department-store shopping was leisured, middle-class, metropolitan. Supermarkets and self-service, the great retailing innovations of the twentieth century, came from the opposite directions. Instead of luxury, they offered functionality and standard products; instead of the pleasures of being served, consumers could congratulate themselves on saving money by doing the work themselves. Food shopping was associated with necessity and routine, whereas department stores had promoted a sense of goods that engendered new desires and possibilities, out of the ordinary. It was the difference between going shopping—an open-ended, pleasurable, perhaps transgressive experience—and doing the shopping, a regular task to be done with the minimum expenditure of time, labor and money.

This distinction though can be problematic in that many go to the supermarket for the entertainment quality that is inherent there. Bowlby recognizes this more in the realm of leisure.[34]

What major department stores do today, as far as grand themes, was something that many did in the past. Often oriented around seasonal festivals, but equally prevalent around special themes, a variety of focuses oriented the store around some kind of exhibition. The famous white sale was already a significant spectacle at the Bon Marche when Zola was researching his *Ladies Delight*. On a more significant scale, what Bloomindgales and Harrods have been doing in a large way in recent years, the full-fledged extravaganzas, were popular at the turn of the century and directly influenced by the exhibitions and expositions that were held every few years on both sides of the Atlantic. "Departments stores regularly mounted special events to coincide with exhibitions."[35]

The former chair of Bloomingdales, Marvin Traub, consciously set out to make Bloomingdale's an entertainment emporium. Buyers, merchandisers, and sponsors all got together to produce themed "extravaganzas" such as "India: The Ultimate Fantasy" and "China: Heralding the Dawn of a New Era."[36] Like many great merchandise impresarios, what influenced his desire to make his store into an entertainment venue were the products of entertainment he engaged with as a youth. The films he saw and the theater he watched had an enormous impact in transforming his store into a stage of retail consumption. The linkages between the theater and mass entertainment are still strong over one hundred years later. Traub feels that entertainment was a "great education for being a merchant." In order to recapture the exciting feelings he felt when he visited the great movie palaces, one now has to go to a store like Bloomingdale's. "To feel that same sense of wonder today," he writes, "you no longer go to Times Square, instead, you go shopping."[37]

Harrods also utilized large displays, "extraordinary exhibitions," especially in its Central Hall. France was profiled in 1990, complete with a large ice model of the Eiffel Tower and cooking demonstrations by some of France's most distinguished chefs. A significant amount of space was also devoted to "A Grand Tour of Italy," held later that same year.[38] To some extent, this is what grand department stores do best. People go to department stores to see unique goods and be entertained by their presentation and display. This is one of the unique aspects inherent within department stores.

A variation on this has been found in stores that specialize in a selection of goods but that are not necessarily department stores. Tiffany & Co., the New York jeweler and purveyor of silver and other precious items, features a wide array of entertainment options that people willingly go to see. Obviously, the landmark Fifth Avenue store, featured in countless films, most notably *Breakfast at Tiffany's*, is itself a tourist attraction and a heritage feature. But within, people are drawn to peruse and just to see. In one significant case, as the designer of the Super Bowl trophy, the artifact was on display—and people ventured inside to see. The same effect is in place with Steuben Glass on Madison Avenue. People canvas the cases and the vases as if they were in a museum. This feature, which has been incorporated into many department stores, reinforces the entertainment component in a very defined and staid manner. One can simply come into a store to see a selection of goods and products just as one could enter a museum or gallery. The famous William Ashley store in Toronto holds just that type of appeal to fans of Baccarat crystal and other fine artifacts.

One of the most damaging developments to traditional department store retailing that has occurred over the past ten years has been the challenge from large retail marketers such as Wal-Mart and Target. Their pull has been so strong that traditional department stores have not been sure how to respond. The large—actually gargantuan—discount arms, CostCo and Sam's Place, have, to some extent appropriated some of their fantasy elements in the form of hugeness, crowds, and free samples, but they do not possess the magic of many established retail emporiums. Consumers, according to Lauren Foster, want a "more engaging shopping experience." What Foster means is that in order for department stores to survive, they must return to their roots as entertainment-retail environments. The notion of experience must be brought back. Utilizing the glamour, art and cultural appeal that was once a significant part of going to a department store, is the only way to recapture the image of old. In an article on the challenges facing traditional department stores, Foster uses Selfridges' as an example for all to emulate. Selfridges' has utilized performance art, celebrity appearances, sculpture and innovative design to resuscitate the proven model of the past. The current CEO of Selfridges', Peter Williams is quoted in the article as saying, "We are trying to assault every one's senses in as many ways as we can. We're in the entertainment business to some extent. It is not just the other retailers that we are competing with. We are competing for leisure time." Other retailers, such as Marshall Fields and

Bloomingdale's are following in the path of Selfridge's. They are trying to redo their stores and offer all the entertainment necessities that make people want to come back to the excitement of the early establishments.[39]

One way to gauge the success and resilience of the department store idea is to look at the flagship stores of a major city. In Paris, the area near the Opera is bounded by a number of large department stores that have a very distinguished lineage and that have been around for many years. The atmosphere in front of and around the Galeries Lafayette is festive, busy, almost carnivalesque. Hundreds, if not thousands, of people—and not nearly as many tourists as one would think—are going in and out, sitting in the department store's coffee shops, looking at the street vendors' gadgets, all suggestive of a circus of consumption. Trying to go into Saks Fifth Avenue in New York in the middle of the day suggests that people are attracted to department stores for something that other retail establishments cannot offer. And of course, Bloomingdales and Harrods remain places for people to go. It is thrilling to people watch on a perch outside any of these establishments.

It is these flagship and often upscale department stores that seem to be able to withstand the challenges. Nordstrom has positioned itself as a luxury oriented department store, with a significant emphasis on service. Simply entering a Nordstrom is entertaining in itself. It is clear, luscious, elegant, and the sales staff are not only knowledgeable but extraordinary in their attempts to serve the customer. It has remained a competitive and popular department store.[40] One of the ways the department stores will survive is by going back to their roots as palaces of luxury. By focusing on prestige items, service and elegance, the upscale department store has become akin to the spa, where the customer is pampered, indulged, and entertained.[41]

One respondent to a series of questions suggested that when he and his wife traveled, whether for business or pleasure, they often went to the traditional department stores located in whatever city they happened to be. He stated that he was quite happy to let his wife roam and shop while he sat down on a bench or a chair and watched people. This aspect of shopping as an entertainment experience was an often-cited reason for men going with their wives. He commented that at the upscale department stores, such as Bloomingdales, this was intensely entertaining. His wife was quick to point out that that was where they first saw the Ralph Lauren Home Collection. "It was the first place that I saw what I'd seen in magazine ads. It was thrilling, like walking through a museum. I got to touch the beds, the linens, the lamps. Such luxury was thrilling."

Whereas the luxury element of traditional department stores is one way in which they will survive, an almost hybrid-like element exists in the Target chain. Although it has been around since the early 1960s, Target came into vogue in a big way in the early 1990s. It became a very important and widely discussed retail outlet that appealed to a broad cross-section of shoppers. What is essentially unique about Target is that it offers its customers a distinct selection of one-of-a-kind goods that are very affordable. The style and sophistication of the products, which range from Tupperware containers, to Sony stereos to Michael Graves houseware, is so cutting-edge and hip, that the trendy shopper rushes in to get them. He, or usually a she, must make an almost weekly pilgrimage to the store in order to ensure that they get these unique items. They are worn, talked about, complimented and given away as gifts.[42]

Target's strategy reflects a concern for content and a respect for the customer. One of the ways in which this comes out is in the philosophy, best described as subtle. Target is oriented around making the customer relax and feel good, not rushed and flustered. The wide width of the aisles, the bright, well-lit stores, the clean and dusted products, all add up to "deepening a relationship" with the customer. It resembles a department store in many ways; the merchandise may be displayed differently, but there is more selection. There is a wealth of distinctive products and smartly designed exclusives, but it is very inexpensive to buy these things. People come back and demonstrate a loyalty because going to Target is fun and entertaining.[43]

Regardless if it is true and unique luxury items, with impeccable service, or mass-produced faux luxury items that are fun to buy, the department store still shows enormous flexibility and resiliency. In many parts of the world, department stores have become much more than emporiums of exchange or cathedrals of consumption. One could go so far as to recognize them on par with other institutions—as being "embedded in culture, reflecting cultural predispositions" and serving as unique transmitters of social life at key historical times.[44] If there is any doubt about this, one must ask someone older about his or her memories of a particular department store. One can also find numerous studies on individual department stores and many references to these places in memoirs. Related to this is the notion that the department store takes on some other set of qualities: an ephemeral set of characteristics that are truly unique.

In the SEED department stores of Japan, a complex array of meanings permeates the store and in turn, have an impact on the consumer. Although it has been argued that Japanese society is extraordinarily different than North American and European society, some interesting parallels can be discerned. As Japan began to take on more Western characteristics, elements of both Eastern and Western society merged. In some instances, one is dominant, while in others there is synergy. SEED goes to extreme lengths to entertain its customers, through the use of design, theater and play, but also, the department store attempts to engage the consumer on a philosophical level that is inherently appealing to the Japanese customer.[45]

It is important to recognize, as has Bill Lancaster, that changes in retailing are constant. The department store was often considered a key institution in this development especially for approximately one hundred and fifty years.[46] The evolution of the department store as an entertainment venue will continue.

NOTES

1. William Leach, *Land of Desire: Merchants, Power, and the Rise of a New American Culture* (New York: Pantheon, 1993), 20.

2. Michael B. Miller, *The Bon Marche: Bourgeois Culture and the Department Store, 1869–1920* (Princeton: Princeton University Press, 1981), 24.

3. Bill Lancaster, *The Department Store: A Social History* (London: Leicester University Press, 1995), 17, 18.

4. Pamela Klaffke, *Spree: A Cultural History of Shopping* (Vancouver: Arsenal Pulp Press, 2003), 46, 47, and Erika Diane Rappaport, *Shopping For Pleasure: Women In the Making of London's West End* (Princeton, N.J.: Princeton University Press, 2000), 5.

5. See Jon Hannigan, "The Global Entertainment Economy," in *Street Protests and Fantasy Parks*, eds. David R. Cameron and Janice Gross Stein (Vancouver: University of British Columbia Press, 2002), 20–48.

6. Rosalynd Williams, *Dream Worlds: Mass Consumption in Late Nineteenth-Century France* (Berkeley: University of California Press, 1986), excerpt in David Crowley and Paul Heyer, *Communication in History*, Third Edition (New York: Longman, 1999) 166–167.

7. Neil Harris, *Cultural Excursions: Marketing Appetites and Cultural Tastes in Modern America* (Chicago: University of Chicago Press, 1990), 184.

8. Erika Diane Rappaport, *Shopping For Pleasure: Women In the Making of London's West End*, 4.

9. Jennifer Jones, "'Coquettes' and 'Grisettes': Women Buying and Selling in Ancien Regime Paris," 32–34.

10. Rachel Bowlby, *Carried Away* (New York: Columbia University Press, 2001), 26, 27.

11. Rachel Bowlby, *Carried Away*, 63, 64.

12. Michael Miller, *The Bon Marche: Bourgeois Culture and the Department Store, 1869–1920* (Princeton, N.J.: Princeton University Press, 1981), 167.

13. Miller, *The Bon Marche*, 167.

14. Miller, *The Bon Marche*, 167. In the introduction to Emile Zola's definitive tale of the workings of a Parisian department store, *Au Bonheur Des Dames* (*The Ladies' Delight*) (London: Penguin, [1883] 2001), Robin Buss writes: "But with the arrival of the large department store, shopping became one of the middle-class woman's chief activities, as well as a recreation and entertainment: the store was a theatre in which the goods were set out in alluring tableaux, the customer was part of the audience for all that the store had to offer." xxii.

15. See Sean Callery, *Harrods Knightsbridge: The Story of Society's Favourite Store* (London: Ebury Press, 1991).

16. Brent Shannon, "ReFashioning Men: Fashion, Masculinity, and the Cultivation of the Male Consumer in Britain, 1860–1914," *Victorian Studies* 46, no. 4 (Summer 2004): 611.

17. Leon Harris, *Merchant Princes* (New York: Harper & Row, 1979), 73.

18. Leon Harris, *Merchant Princes*, 74. Italics in the original.

19. Erika Diane Rappaport, *Shopping For Pleasure: Women In the Making of London's West End* (Princeton, N.J.: Princeton University Press, 2000), 155.

20. Erika Diane Rappaport, *Shopping For Pleasure*, 161.

21. Erika Diane Rappaport, *Shopping For Pleasure*, 162.

22. William Lancaster, *The Department Store: A Social History* (London: Leicester University Press, 1995), 5.

23. Erika Diane Rappaport, *Shopping For Pleasure*, 178.

24. See Meredith L. Clausen, "The Department Store—Development of a Type," *Journal of Architectural Education* (Washington, D.C.: Association of Collegiate Schools of Architecture, Fall 1985), 20–29, cited in *Servicescapes: The Concept of Place in Contemporary Markets*, ed. John F. Sherry Jr. (Chicago: NTC Business Books, 1998).

25. Leach, *Land of Desire*.

26. Miller, *The Bon Marche*, 167–69.

27. Leach, *Land of Desire*, 23.

28. Leach, *Land of Desire*, 57–60, 70, 102, 103, and James B. Twitchell, *Lead Us Into Temptation: The Triumph of American Materialism* (New York: Columbia University Press, 1999), 235.

29. Neil Harris, *Cultural Excursions: Marketing Appetites and Cultural Tastes in Modern America* (Chicago: University of Chicago Press, 1990), 63.

30. Harris, *Cultural Excursions*, 65.

31. Leach, *Land of Desire*, 136.

32. Harris, *Cultural Excursions*, 65.

33. Ann Satterthwaite, *Going Shopping: Consumer Choices and Community Consequences* (New Haven/London: Yale University Press, 2001), 43.

34. Bowlby, *Carried Away*, 5, 8.

35. Geoffrey Crossick and Serge Jaumain, "The World of the Department Store: Distribution, Culture and Social Exchange," in *Cathedrals of Consumption: The European Department Store, 1850–1939*, eds. Geoffrey Crossick and Serge Jaumain (Aldershot, UK: Ashgate, 1999), 28.

36. Marvin Traub (and Tom Teicholz), *Like No Other Store: The Bloomingdale's Legend and the Revolution in American Marketing* (New York: Random House, 1993), xiv.

37. Traub (and Teicholz), *Like No Other Store*, 12, 13.

38. Callery, *Harrods Knightsbridge*, 156.

39. Lauren Foster, "Department Stores Must Adapt or Die," *The Financial Post* (Friday, December 26, 2003), FP8.

40. Ellen Byron, "Nordstrom Regains Its Luster," *The Wall Street Journal* (August 19, 2004), B.2.

41. Steve McLinden, "On The Rebound," *Shopping Centers Today* (New York: International Council of Shopping Centers, August 2004), http://www.icsc.org/srch/sct/sct0804/cover_2.shtml.

42. Laura Rowley, *On Target: How the World's Hottest Retailer Hit a Bull's-Eye* (New Jersey: John Wiley and Sons, 2003), 2–13.

43. Rowley, *On Target*, 9–13.

44. Millie Creighton, "The Seed of Creative Lifestyle Shopping: Wrapping Consumerism in Japanese Store Layouts," in *Servicescapes*, ed. Sherry Jr., 203.

45. Creighton, "The Seed of Creative Lifestyle Shopping," 205–206.

46. Lancaster, *The Department Store*, 3.

4

✛

The Mall

The notion of "going to the mall" as a way to satisfy an entertainment need was built upon the layers of leisure, which had expanded in every way and form after the Second World War. By the 1970s, the mall was a ubiquitous feature of the suburban wilderness, a key pinpoint in the edge cities that sprouted up in regions just outside urban centers. With no downtown core, and inadequate strip stores, the mall, as defined by Victor Gruen, became a focal point for a variety of different activities. The mall was designed to mimic or recreate the city or the town, complete with a main thoroughfare, side streets, gathering places, fountains, and central meeting areas.[1] What inspired Gruen was not just the European town square and market, but, as well, the impressive sites he saw as a new immigrant to New York. It was not the massive and impressive skyscrapers, but importantly, Broadway or "the Great White Way" and Central Park. Constructed for totally different reasons yet similar in the fact that both provided "entertainment for all comers," these two New York features were to have an important influence in his later shopping mall designs.[2]

Gruen consciously set out to recreate the best of what the old downtown had to offer, in essence making the mall a "crystallization point" for shoppers and for the community at large. In contrast to the "ugliness" of the aging downtown cores, complete with crime and poverty, the new "shopping town" was supposed to do away with all the unpleasantries and create or recreate the best of the old system. This of course included bringing in as many shoppers as possible.[3] And to a great extent, Gruen's ideas succeeded.

Gruen recognized many important qualities that have come to be part and parcel of mall culture. Selling or retail, for Gruen, was an environment that "could entertain Americans better than any show, exhibition, or performance. In all of his designs," writes M. Jeffrey Hardwick, "he relied on visual surprises to amuse visitors, create consumers, and produce profits." Hardwick suggests that Gruen employed a variety of tactics to make shopping an entertaining experience. "Using artificial lights, giant show windows, and fancy facades for his stores—grand fountains, twirling sculptures, and rose gardens for his shopping centers—Gruen attempted to seduce and produce a larger audience for retailers."[4]

Like Walter Benjamin's stroller in the arcades, one could casually walk through or down these new urban "arcades" and see and be seen. This would quickly take the place of the urban window shopper as well as the *flaneur*. The mall also quickly became the surrogate public gathering place. Two early malls in New Jersey took on the roles of being "central sites of consumption," offering even more than would have been available in the downtown core. Both the Garden State Plaza and the Bergen Mall had numerous entertainment and leisure offerings, which included movie theaters, bowling alleys, skating rinks, playgrounds, and meeting rooms for community organizations. Like the grand department stores, sponsored cultural, artistic, and educational programs, which involved lectures and information evenings to the point that one observer has concluded that both malls positioned themselves as central focuses of their communities.[5]

Malls have come to be much more than consumption sites. Studies suggest that many people simply go to the mall rather than go anywhere else. The mall attracts shoppers, but also, and importantly, browsers, people looking to get something to eat, exercise walkers, and those simply there to engage in some kind of social connection. Of this latter group, numerous people come to the mall simply to watch other people. The mall has become an enormously entertaining place and has become one of the most entertaining environments for many people.[6]

Paul Lukas, commenting on both Gruen and Hardwick's book on Gruen, observes that the development of the first suburban malls in the United States, Northland and in particular Southdale, came at roughly the same time as Walt Disney opened Disneyland. Lukas intimates that one of Disney's key attractions was "Main Street USA," which "mimicked a downtown business district just as Southdale" had done. Disney himself wanted to erase the unpleasant elements that shoppers often experience. All the messiness was eradicated. There was no crime, no bad weather, no homeless desperados begging for money, no parking problems. What is significant here though is the fact that both Gruen and Disney were in the dream business. According to Disney, "I want them to feel they are in another world." The mall environment recreates and reinforces this intention. Malls, to some extent, have become dream places: entertainment environments where theme parks and amusement blend seamlessly.[7] Commenting on the above, one respondent stated, "You know the Willy Wonka Chocolate Factory in the movie? It is completely fantastic. That's how I feel when I enter a mall." But both Disney culture and mall worlds have realistic concerns that must be dealt with, even though they are often hidden.

Ample parking also made the suburban mall extremely appealing. One has to be aware of how important this became to the movement of people—shoppers—from the city to the suburbs. At the heart of the expansion of the malls was the ability to not only move large numbers of people, but also allow them access in a way that was becoming impossible in the downtown core. This unique American innovation, the large suburban mall, was made possible by a coalition of factors, but space was the primary motivating reason for the American mall. Witold Rybcsynski has suggested that this was a significant American mind-set originating in the Colonial period. The availability of land and the desire to spread out influenced the design and building of the mall.[8]

It is important to acknowledge, as does Mark Gottdiener, that the first malls were not competing against each other, as they do today. They had to market themselves as something different from the downtown shopping districts and in particular the large urban department stores. One of the reasons why malls sought to distinguish themselves both through advertising and atmosphere was to attract "potential customers." Malls often adopt themes or motifs that infuse the mall—its interior and its design—with an image that can attract customers. This competition and this desire to stand apart, accounts for many of the entertainment qualities that have infused malls.[9] And these devices have been quite successful. People flock to the mall in order to do many things, beyond shopping.

Whether one hates to acknowledge this or not, the mall today is where people gather, and not just in inclement weather. The mall provides close parking for mothers with small children and encourages seniors to come and walk through the mall in the early morning hours. Many community activities, such as fund-raising, now take place in the mall.[10] At what is often touted "Canada's Flagship Mall," Yorkdale Shopping Centre, the gathering of retired men is a common occurrence. They congregate in groups of up to 15, walk around, have something to eat, and go on with their day. Despite the often-labeled criticism that malls are not the same as the town square, their role as a community meeting place has grown and is now acknowledged. "They reflect the suburban values of society. And they're increasingly becoming entertainment vehicles," in the opinion of at least one scholar.[11]

Mall developers are aware that many of the people who frequent malls do not necessarily come there with the specific intention to shop. As malls have become dominant public or community gathering places, they attract people, often for the simple reason that there is nowhere else to go. And within their environs, there are a host of attractions. The bottom line is that even though these people did not decide to come and shop, most of them end up buying something.[12] Malls also exhibit a remarkable degree of resiliency, the ability to adapt and to evolve. For every stale mall that closes, a sophisticated new shopping experience arises not too far away. Malls, like department stores, can and will survive if they are capable of adapting.[13]

The mall is where people now go to spend time; teenagers hang out at the mall instead of cruising the strip.[14] As Margaret Crawford details, the WEM and other super malls, such as the Mall of America in Minnesota, resemble small cities that are in many cases open almost twenty-four hours. These environments, with their enormous workforces, can contain or offer virtually every service from chapels to hotels. Condensing all of one's needs and consumer desires into one place heightens the need for the merging of entertainment, shopping, and leisure. Simply put, if you build it, people will come.[15]

A significant fact in the internal design of malls over the last few years is that more and more space has been allocated for the traditional "entertainment" aspect of leisure. Whereas in their earliest inception and during their adolescence, malls had either a *de facto* entertainment element or stores themselves featured entertainment components, increasingly malls have created specific entertainment zones as well as retail-tainment sites. As shopping guru Paco Underhill writes, "Once upon a time, a dank little video game arcade was considered sufficient. Today malls have taken on a lot of the burden of keeping suburban America diverted."[16] The most prosaic reason for this is centered on the fact that those who are not there for shopping will at least 'hang around' in the mall if there is something to do. From teenagers to men in general, offering entertainment outlets is useful as a diversion. Interestingly, according to Underhill, going to the mall has become an activity that is not necessarily focused on shopping. "People may now come to the mall," he writes, "without intending to buy a single thing." Whether it is to hang out or to socialize, an important reason to visit the mall is the vague desire "to have fun."[17]

The idea of "having fun" is not a trivial explanation. Mall developers and retailers take this seemingly innocent idea and think about it. "Having fun" means many things including increased profits, but it is an approach that is tied to shopping as an entertainment experience. As one journalist has written, "Consumers are frequenting shopping centers for more than just the latest merchandise. They are coming to have a good time as well. That is fine with the retail industry, which recently has become obsessed with entertaining its customers."[18] The definition of "being entertained" is infinite in its possibilities. As Matthew Haeberle implies, it could mean seeing a favorite musician or meeting a local beauty queen; playing hockey at the mall or being wowed at a specific store display; seeing a fashion show or watching a cooking display. Developers and mall managers see this as icing on the cake, in the sense that selling or retail should come first.[19] But the industry knows that it must do something different all the time in order to keep people coming in. "Dramatically different" is the operative phrase, whether it is in the super mall category or the historic city center. The envelope for entertainment difference expands as each year passes. In Madrid, Spain, the Mills Corporation opened a large mall and entertainment complex. The mall's distinguishing feature as far as entertainment options goes, was a huge snow dome, where consumers could ski and snowboard—all year round.[20] "As entertaining as possible" is the new dictum.[21]

The mall has much in common with the casino as well as the carnival. Besides its liminal evocation, there are practical comparisons. One often loses track of time in the mall. This is common in many artificial environments, and like the casino, clocks are largely absent. The suspension or nullification of time, and concern for time, has many ramifications. Most significantly, it is a true hallmark of carefree leisure. Simply not caring how long one is in a particular place is suggestive of true freedom. Not knowing what the weather is like outside or what time of day it is, is evocative of the mind-set of one on vacation. At one and the same time it is "disorienting" and "insulating."[22]

Like the WEM, the Mall of America in Bloomington, Minnesota, is a huge entertainment/tourist attraction, drawing more visitors than Disney World, Graceland, and the Grand Canyon combined.[23] Michelle Lee describes the environment at the Mall of America as being essentially composed of the same stores that one would find at any other well-endowed mall. Yet what makes the Mall of America unique, beyond it size, is its full-fledged adoption of the entertainment ethos. "Its true selling point," she writes,

> is entertainment—too many attractions to list. Among them: a twenty-six-ride amusement park with Ferris wheel and roller coaster, bowling alley, shark tank, eight nightclubs, eighteen-hole mini-golf course, a college campus, and twenty-seven fast-food restaurants.[24]

Even if one is absolutely against the whole idea of shopping at malls, there is always a mall that will appeal to that individual. Regardless of political or philosophic viewpoints, the mall, in the words of Robert Wilson, fascinates. Wilson writes even those who "despise" the mall and the mall experience will inevitably view the mall idea as "compelling" in some way.[25] Significant in this process is Victor Gruen's original idea for the mall. Beyond the fact that one is in an enclosed, climate-controlled environment, one is a captive destined to roam, originally the large pedestrian space between the then two anchor stores. The more appealing and pleasing the environment, the more likely one was to stay longer, be happy, and inevitably, purchase something.[26]

One reason that even the most reluctant of consumers will find some element of mall culture appealing may have to do with the process of "indirect commodification." This process implies that anything that enters the mall environment—activities and images—become, by association, reconfigured and tinged with the effects of the mall. Extended, what occurs is the association of the shopping experience with "an intense spectacle of accumulated images and themes that entertain and stimulate and in turn encourage more shopping."[27] This is exactly why one encounters merry-go-rounds, ferris wheels, and a host of other amusements within malls. And, this is also why malls are no longer places for shopping but "highly organized social spaces for entertainment, interaction, and other types of consumer excitement."[28]

A further development of this theme-based approach is found in the redevelopment of places such as Faneuil Hall in Boston and South Street Seaport in New York. Culture is reconfigured to appeal to both entertainment and shopping.[29] These festival marketplaces harness the history of the market and link them with the traditions of city or urban culture. A key element to their entertainment appeal is the interaction of people with novelty, aesthetic pleasure, and a downtown feel. Unique stores in these settings complete their appeal.[30]

Not only is culture reconfigured but so too is nature. At Yonge and Eglinton in midtown Toronto, there is a mall that contains a pet store just outside of a large HMV music store. Parents wait patiently as their children visit the different animals in various cages. Children of all ages try to entice a parrot to speak or hope to hold a little kitten. One parent explained, "this is on our route. Every weekend a stop here keeps them happy." As a surrogate for the zoo, the pet store has one advantage. Children can often touch the animals. This process is summed up appropriately by Underhill:

Even stores can serve as forms of entertainment. Here's one category that's vanishing from malls overall, but can still occasionally be found: pet shops. Selling critters in the mall looks like a labor-intensive, somehow seedy undertaking. Still, go to any mall pet store, and you'll find children gathered around the front windows or the cages inside. It's like a zoo for small domestic animals—puppies, kittens, bunnies, the occasional piglet, all romping inside their too-small cages. It's one of those places parents dread. But five or ten minutes in such a store can restore the spirits of a cranky seven-year-old, thereby making it possible for parents to shop a little longer. Thanks to Animal Planet and the Discovery Channel, we get visually close to animals, but we can't smell or touch them. Even the modern zoo is discovering that closeness to simple domesticated critters like goats, sheep, and ponies is a major draw.[31]

Nature is also reconfigured in a major manner with the use of artificial trees, plants, and water ponds to lend an air of mystery, excitement, or relaxation to the shopping environment. Many malls employ significant numbers of personnel to tend to their indoor jungles. The versions found at the Rainforest Café are just one extreme.

And it is not just the quantity of flora and fauna; it is also the quality. In some sophisticated retail environments, the species available, both in the mall and surrounding the outside rim, are quite rare and very expensive. This is not your garden store variety. Massive aquariums and terrariums that rival even the best offerings of high-profile zoos and major fish repositories often further accent this excessive and impressive display. So successful have malls and other retail environments been at virtually co-opting the traditional sites of nature as artifice, that their attendance has declined and their directors are following the examples of retail environments in order to get back on track.

John Beardsley worries that UnderWater World at the Mall of America, where you pay a fee to see a vast array of marine life, is intensely problematic. He argues that this trend "views and uses nature as a sales gimmick or marketing strategy, often through the production of replicas or simulations." This process, he feels, is "modifying our conceptions of nature."[32] Stores such as The Nature Company and The Body Shop alter one's relationship at one level, while the simulated jungles of the Rainforest Café alter it at another, more forceful level. While entertaining and eye opening, these constructions do not change habits and do not, according to Beardsley, "teach us to be responsible."[33] One must ask, though, does hiking on a mapped-out trail or white water rafting on a river, change, for most people, their habits?

These "buyospheres" have many elements in common with real landscapes except that they are devoid of the problems inherent in the real world. Mall developers know what they are doing and do it very well. The lessons of Disney World and Las Vegas are refined in the mall environment. From courts and avenues, to eating as a cultural experience, to theme nightclubs to atriums, the mall has become the most breathtaking of environments.[34]

Carol Rifkind has written that the mall "setting" is composed of "theatricality, illusion, pretense, manipulation, and artifice."[35] This is one of the most-often-leveled criticisms at mall culture. One reason for the constancy and severity of this critique is that it is so successful at creating an environment that is both manipulative and entertaining. Rifkind makes the point that perhaps the most potent influence on mall development was not the arcade or the department store, but the "turn-of-the-century amusement park." It was in this (originally) safe environment that "innocent pleasures" could be enjoyed. "Like the amusement park," she writes, "the mall is environmental theater, built like stage scenery, and just as easily modified. In the mall, nothing is permitted to appear old or obsolete . . ."[36]

In certain malls, there is a fair amount of sunlight that comes in from a central skylight or a few strategically placed skylights. Most mall developers refuse to use the true outside world in any significant way, one fearing that this may encourage the shopper to want to leave the mall and go elsewhere—to another world.[37] The notion of shopping as theater or "retail drama" kicks in at this point. "The idea," according to Laura Byrne Paquet, "is to replicate the artificial feeling of a theater or a Hollywood sound stage, where shoppers can be the stars of their own show."[38] This concept is carried forth in a phenomenal way; if the shoppers and others are "part of the cast" there is the archway as a stage, and the ability to try on "costumes," touch "props" and in general, engage in the dramatic ritual of shopping.[39]

Newer malls and recently redesigned malls now have full-fledged entertainment attractions beyond traditional movie theaters. Comedy clubs have become a feature in many malls, not to mention a theater or an auditorium for live events. Comedy clubs and other live offerings seem to stimulate the malls, especially in suburban venues.[40] They dovetail quite nicely with restaurants and other ancillary entertainment activities.

Hybrid malls or variations on the traditional covered mall have proven to be both successful and resilient. The definitive versions are places such as Boston's Faneuil Hall or New York's South Street Seaport. These outdoor arcade-like structures harness the appeal of traditional pedestrian areas with the glamour and prestige of history. When they are successful, they draw urban dwellers, tourists, and visitors from the suburbs. They combine the shopping essence of the marketplace with the atmosphere of a fairground. Usually, they are upscale in their offerings and are peppered with fancy restaurants, trendy coffee shops, and are sprinkled with galleries as well as stores. A theater company or playhouse is not an uncommon attraction, as is the case with Toronto's Distillery District. One way to keep the unique balance is to avoid the standard offerings found in traditional malls and tourist venues. That is why many of these "festival marketplaces" go out of their way to attract creative retailers and singular attractions.[41]

The above retail entertainment sites have much in common with historic sites and villages that now include malls of some note. This phenomenon is discussed at greater length in chapter 8. Yet, it is interesting to look at this evolution as a pure variation of the mall. Shopping is now a full-fledged part of historic culture. People often wish to take something away from an historic site in order to remind them of what they saw or perhaps to define the trip or excursion in a tangible way. Colonial Williamsburg appeals, despite its ersatz flavor to those with an interest in American history. Yet front and center in the historic site is a shopping mall. Key to the development of these retail/educational entertainment locales, the malls or clusters of shops provide much-needed capital. Ensconced among "historic" buildings and antiquities, shops, kiosks, and stores, not to mention cafes, all the trappings of the mall are to be found.[42]

One can view this process at work at universities throughout North America. Most major institutions of higher education have some variation of the shopping mall on campus. At York University, at the northern end of Toronto, York Lanes is a miniature version of a shopping mall. At most hours of the day, students and employees of this university city can be found walking through the Lanes, perusing clothing in the stores, playing pool in the arcade, or dining on a variety of foods. At the far end of the mall is the university's bookstore, resembling in many ways, a well-stocked Borders or Indigo.

Another twist on the traditional mall concept is the mall in the airport. Large and new terminals set aside significant shopping areas that appeal to travelers in many ways. Both in the duty-free and general format, no airport redesign and no new airport is complete without a shopping mall. This is a far cry from the limited and expensive offerings that marked their predecessors. Now, whatever can be found at a large suburban mall has its parallel at the airport. Fancy food shops, used book stores, wine stores and high-end gift stores are part of the mix, not to mention entertainment kiosks and quality restaurants. All these offerings are grouped together in a geographic cluster that is convenient and comforting.[43] Travelers who are familiar with a specific airport mall, one with unique shops, will often try to get there early, in order to explore. Some airport malls are even gaining a reputation as prime shopping destinations. No longer is this venue a last-minute place to pick up souvenirs, it is often a retail draw in itself. In certain airports brand-name national designers offer their products, while in others national retailers have stores or sections in stores. Especially attractive to consumers looking for retail stimulation is the new generation of shoppertainment outlets. From the

National Geographic Store in Washington to the Field Museum Store in Chicago, to the Kennedy Space Station Store in Orlando, the creative offerings of these ventures are of great appeal to shoppers.[44]

As malls evolve, certain themes become evident. The notion of entertainment as an aspect of shopping has become paramount in the evolution of the mall. To illustrate how important entertainment is to shopping and as well as how closely connected shopping and entertainment have become, one authority observed that the WEM originally had an 80 percent to 20 percent ratio of retail to entertainment. That figure has now moved in the direction of entertainment. It is now about 60 percent to 40 percent. Perhaps this increase in full-fledged entertainment within the confines of a shopping environment is a response to the rise of Internet and catalogue shopping which challenged the practice of going out to shop to such a degree that it is necessary for traditional shopping venues to "up the ante" in order to survive.[45]

As long as the mall offers something "extraordinary" it is going to draw a crowd. That is why new malls are constructed with entertainment fully in mind. Whether it is the large hybrid malls such as those constructed by the Mills Corporation or the high-end elite malls, shopping, as entertainment remains a key attraction. The Mills Corporation owns and runs onsite television production facilities and video screens offer information and entertainment to customers.[46]

To say that the mall has grown old and stale is not an accurate assessment. Mall culture has become pervasive in contemporary society. The development of ethnic malls, which often reconstruct the shopping environments of home cultures, is becoming a very popular element to some malls, especially in Vancouver and Toronto. Store owners who often own and run the mall sublet and subdivide their spaces in almost booth-like set-ups. This allows for the recreation of environments that are reminiscent of the home cultures, but also allows for a variety of entertainment and social features that are absent from traditional malls. These creations allow for a wide array of traditional festivals and events, such as holiday celebrations and children's cultural performances.[47]

People gravitate to the mall at different times of the day, for different things. Even in such a shopping mecca as Manhattan, the mall is of grand entertainment appeal. The recent opening of the Time Warner Center Mall on the Upper West Side of New York City generated much interest. While some worry about the fact that this new development replicates what is available virtually everywhere, others are excited about the fact that New York City now has its own essential shopping sphere.[48] This new emporium is filled with a mix of familiar and unique stores, grand arcades and all the comfortable and attractive features synonymous with suburbia.

When asked if she still frequented traditional large malls instead of or in conjunction with outlet/big box stores, a middle-aged homemaker replied: "You've got to understand that the feeling I get when I enter Bayview or Yorkdale—when it isn't crowded it's wonderful. I love the smells, I love the excitement and most of all, I love looking in the stores. I can leave my coat in the car and just run in. Just a short time inside, even if I don't buy anything, always fills me with comfort and hope. It's fun and exciting." One reason why the traditional mall will not disappear—although it will evolve—is because of that respondent's sentiments. As malls continue to be more than places to buy, they become, like other retail environments, places to have an experience. They can be satisfying socially, intellectually, and artistically.[49]

Like other aspects of mass consumer and touristic culture, the mall is also a tourist draw. In Toronto, whenever people visit from out of town, there is a specific list of things to see and do. These usually include visits to certain neighborhoods, the CN Tower, the Royal Ontario Museum, perhaps the Art Gallery of Ontario, and maybe the Ontario Science Center. One place that is always included on the agenda is the Eaton Centre. What makes the Eaton Centre so unique is the fact that it is an extremely large downtown mall, anchored by two department stores. It is situated on the most famous of Toronto's streets and is essentially a large-scale atrium-like structure built around an existing church. Within its confines spaces on various levels allow people to walk through. On the top floor, a glass roof is derivative of both Milan's Galleria Vittorio Emanuele II as well as Paxton's Crystal Palace.[50] Artist Michael Snow's famous *Geese* sculpture dominates one end of the mall. The center is extremely busy and often, quite crowded with shoppers and those just wandering.

In regions with extreme climates, such as the very cold—Minneapolis, Toronto, Montreal—or the very hot and humid—Houston, Miami—the mall will retain its appeal. Shoppers and mall browsers appreciate an environment that makes them feel comfortable and to where they can go for a leisurely walk.[51] As well, certain environments, notably colder one's, such as in Toronto and in Montreal, have both pioneered and perfected, the underground mall. In Toronto miles of pedestrian walkways link shops and underground malls. These cater to people working in office towers above the malls, and are filled with shoppers, primarily during lunchtime and after work hours. On the weekends, they are dead spaces, vast canyons of marble and harsh lighting, devoid of people.[52]

Developers know why people like the malls and are responding in kind. Both retailers and developers are aware that the customer who goes to the mall generally wishes to be there for a while. He or she is not just dashing in for some essential item. And they are trying to reward that commitment. Obviously, the bottom line is to get the consumer to purchase, but making the environment as attractive as possible is now key. Addressing the needs of many consumers is also significant.[53]

With its open-air art gallery, new cars, and opulent surroundings, the Time Warner Center Mall is only one of many malls that have a specific entertainment focus and relationship. The rise of the entertainment mall is increasingly tied to its developers, media corporations. Sony pioneered this process, investing heavily in entertainment malls that are saturated with media products and come complete with the ubiquitous television screens and electronic games. Whether in Germany or San Francisco, or Universal Studios and its City Walk, the merging is significant.[54]

All this is exactly what people have come to expect. The sense of newness, freshness, and the overall appeal of enticements now found in the typical mall, accentuated by lighting and design, is hugely exciting. But with its deep, familiar historical references, is comforting as well. Developers, architects, and designers have now taken this a step further.

NOTES

1. Aaron Betsky, "All the World's a Store: The Spaces of Shopping," in *Brand.new*, ed. Jane Pavitt (Princeton, N.J.: Princeton University Press, 2000), 126, and Margaret Crawford, "Suburban Life and Public Space," in *Sprawl and Public Space: Redressing the Mall*, ed. Donald J. Smiley (New York: Princeton Architectural Press/National Endowment for the Arts, 2002), 22–25.

2. M. Jeffrey Hardwick, *Mall Maker: Victor Gruen, Architect of an American Dream* (Philadelphia: University of Pennsylvania Press, 2004), 16.

3. Lizabeth Cohen, *A Consumer's Republic: The Politics of Mass Consumption in Postwar America* (New York: Knopf, 2003), 261–263.

4. M. Jeffrey Hardwick, *Mall Maker*, 4.

5. Lizabeth Cohen, *A Consumer's Republic* (New York: Vintage, 2003), 263, 264.

6. See the studies quoted in Ozlem Sandikci and Douglas B. Holt, "Malling Society: Mall Consumption Practices and the Future of Public Space," in *Servicescapes: The Concept of Place in Contemporary Markets*, ed. John F. Sherry Jr. (Chicago: NTC Business Books, 1998), 306.

7. Paul Lukas, "Our Malls, Ourselves," *Fortune* 150, no. 18 (October 18, 2004) 243–45.

8. See Witold Rybczynski, *City Life: Urban Expectations In a New World* (Toronto: HarperCollins, 1995).

9. Mark Gottdiener, "The Semiotics of Consumer Spaces," in *Servicescapes: The Concept of Place in Contemporary Markets*, ed. John F. Sherry Jr. (Chicago: NTC Business Books, 1998), 37, 38.

10. Betsky, "All the World's a Store," 126.

11. Cited in Marina Strauss, "Canada's Flagship Yorkdale Mall Has a Life All Its Own," *The Globe and Mail* (December 20, 2003), B1.

12. Ira G. Zepp Jr., *The New Religious Image of Urban America: The Shopping Mall as Ceremonial Center*, Second Edition (Niwot: University Press of Colorado, 1997), 66.

13. Phillip Langdon, "The Evolution of Shopping," *The American Enterprise* 11, no. 2 (March 2000), 45–36.

14. Margaret Crawford, "The World in a Shopping Mall," in *Variations on a Theme Park: The New American City and the End of Public Space*, ed. Michael Sorkin (New York: The Noonday Press, 1992), 15.

15. Crawford, "The World in a Shopping Mall," 6, 15.

16. Paco Underhill, *Call of the Mall* (New York: Simon & Schuster, 2004), 85.

17. Underhill, *Call of the Mall*, 87.

18. Matthew Haeberle, "Center Stage at the Mall," *Chain Store Age* 77, no. 6 (June 2001), 128.

19. Haeberle, "Center Stage at the Mall," 128.

20. Albert Warson, "More Excitement, Please," *Building* 53, no. 6 (December 1, 2003), 4.

21. Sunil Taneja, "Reinventing the Experience," *Chain Store Age* 74, no. 11 (November 1998), 153.

22. Russel W. Belk and Wendy Bryce, "Christmas Shopping Scenes: From Modern Miracle to Postmodern Mall," *International Journal of Research in Marketing* 10 (1993), 288.

23. Michelle Lee, *Fashion Victim: Our Love-Hate Relationship with Dressing, Shopping and the Cost of Style* (New York: Broadway Books, 2003), xix.

24. Lee, *Fashion Victim*, 75.

25. Robert R. Wilson, "Playing and Being Played: Experiencing West Edmonton Mall," in *Pop Can: Popular Culture in Canada*, eds. Lynne Van Luven and Priscilla L. Walton (Scarborough, ON: Prentice Hall, 1999), 83.

26. Gabian Faurholt Csaba and Soren Askegaard, "Malls and the Orchestration of the Shopping Experience in a Historical Perspective," *Advances in Consumer Research*, vol. 26 (1999), 35.

27. Crawford, "The World in a Shopping Mall," 15, 16.

28. A. F. Firat and A. Venkatesh, "Postmodernity: The Age of Marketing," *International Journal of Research in Marketing* 10, no. 3 (1993) 233.

29. Crawford, "The World in a Shopping Mall," 16, 17.

30. Michael J. Bednar, *Interior Pedestrian Places* (New York: Whitney Library of Design, 1989), 93–95.

31. Underhill, *Call of the Mall*, 88.

32. John Beardsley, "Kiss Nature Goodbye," *Harvard Design Magazine* 10 (Winter/Spring 2000), 1.

33. Beardsley, "Kiss Nature Goodbye," 2–4. Beardsley writes on page 3: . . . the chief product of the Body Shop and the Nature Company is irony, albeit unintended. These boutiques promise to help us get in touch with nature, but instead they effectively remove us from it . . . The larger environment of the mall likewise exploits our affection for nature in order to soothe us in the act of consumption."

34. Lee, *Fashion Victim*, 90–91.

35. Carole Rifkind, "America's Fantasy Urbanism: The Waxing of the Mall and the Waning of Civility," in *Dumbing Down: Essays on the Strip-Mining of American Culture,* eds. Katharine Washburn and John Thornton (New York: Norton, 1996), 262.

36. Rifkind, "America's Fantasy Urbanism," 264–65.

37. Laura Byrne Paquet, *The Urge To Splurge: A Social History of Shopping* (Toronto: ECW Press, 2003), 99.

38. Paquet, *The Urge To Splurge,* 99.

39. Paquet, *The Urge To Splurge,* 99.

40. Maura K. Ammenheuser, "And That's No Joke," *Shopping Centers Today* (July 2004), http://wwwicsc.org/srch/sct/set0704/rt_1shtml.

41. Susan Thorne, "Area Re-Spirited," *Shopping Centers Today* (June 2004), http://www.icsc.org/srch/sct/sct0604/page25.html.

42. Ian Ritter, "Old Town, New Shops," *Shopping Centers Today* (July 2003), http://www.icsc.org/srch/sct/sct0703/page15.html.

43. Steve McLinden, "Happier Landings," *Shopping Centers Today* (January 2004), http://www.icsc.org/srch/sct/set0104/page13.html.

44. Steve McLinden, "Airports Looking More and More Like Top-End Malls," *Shopping Centers Today* (January 2004), http://www.icsc.org/srch/sct/set0104/pagela.html.

45. Cited in George Ritzer, *Enchanting a Disenchanted World,* Second Edition (Thousand Oaks, Calif.: Pine Forge, 2005), 118.

46. Langdon, "The Evolution of Shopping," 35, 36.

47. Margaret Crawford, "Suburban Life and Public Space," in *Sprawl and Public Spaces: Redressing the Mall* eds. David Smiley (New York: Princeton Architectural Press, 200), 30.

48. Steven Edwards, "In New York, Not All Want To Mall," *The National Post* (Wednesday, February 18, 2004), A13.

49. See James J. Farrell, *One Nation under Goods: Malls and the Seductions of American Shopping* (Washington, D.C.: Smithsonian, 2003), 182.

50. Michael J. Bednar, *Interior Pedestrian Places* (New York: Whitney Library of Design, 1989), 59–60.

51. Bednar, *Interior Pedestrian Places,* 26.

52. See Robert Fulford, "Tunnel Vision," *Toronto Life* (January 1993), 29–31.

53. Sunil Taneja, "Reinventing the Experience," *Chain Store Age* 74, no. 11 (November 1998), 153–55.

54. Crawford, "Surburban Life and Public Space," 26.

5

The E-Store

Throughout the post-World-War-Two period, a shift in public amusement occurred that pushed what was once a mainstay of outdoor amusements into two distinct spheres. One of these manifestations was the indoor mall, while the other was the home.

As a result of television, movie attendance declined. Numerous gimmicks were introduced to lure back moviegoers, ranging from the drive-in to wide-screen formats. Yet the public seemed content to sit at home and watch television. In the United States what was once a very vibrant collection of entertainment activities, from amusement parks to theater, disappeared. A significant reason for this decline aside from television was the rapid move of many people away from major city areas that had lively public amusements to the suburbs.

By the 1970s and the early 1980s, sitting at home, "cocooning," was a major entertainment focus. Home theater, the VCR, and other new technologies made it very easy to *not* go out. This process began in the 1950s and reached a critical point in the late 1970s and early 1980s. Sony introduced miniature televisions while the development and marketing of the VCR allowed people to control what was once a major obstacle in visual entertainment activities. Video games and video game devices accentuated the attractions of staying at home. A new kind of solitary individualism took over that made more people comfortable with personal entertainment outlets and stalled the kinds of social interactions that had previously been in place.[1]

Retailers and other interested parties were concerned about this focus, especially in the evening hours, and sought ways to reinvigorate going out and to combine it with a supreme shopping experience.[2] According to a group of authors composed primarily of members of the American Urban Land Institute's project on retail entertainment,

> Several generations of Americans have now grown up in a largely homogeneous suburban environment, and they are looking for something more. For consumers who have been everywhere, seen everything, and done everything, the old entertainment options simply will not do. People are becoming blase about the technological wizardry that is available to them at home and at work. And the old-style shopping mall, the epicenter of suburban culture and entertainment, is dull when compared with the promise of a spectacular collection of new, out-of-home retail and entertainment options that, if creatively bundled and executed, can capture the interest of the most jaded guest.[3]

This has led to the creation of an entity known as "retail entertainment development" that has a number of fundamental factors. These are "pure entertainment attractions" such as cinemas, "theme restaurants," and "entertainment-oriented shops."[4] The variations are endless and the mixes are varied. In some instances, these are located in suburban areas, while in many examples they are part of what was once called urban renewal. In some cases these developments are partnered up with existing cultural or sporting concerns while other variants stand alone.

It is important to note that the design, construction, and maintenance of shopping environments incorporate numerous elements of attraction and entertainment. Some of these are subtle, but most are quite obvious. Malls, for example, have a tendency to show wear on a level akin to hotel rooms. Quickly, they become worn down, tarnished and dull. The ideal maintenance of the mall environment means keeping everything shiny and polished, new and kept-up. Nothing is more depressing to a prospective shopper than a dull and dingy environment. In particular, artificial lighting magnifies defects and decay. Greenery and natural lighting, high ceilings, and the presence of highly polished surfaces, such as mirrors, and shining chrome and clean glass, greatly accelerate positive feelings. People come to these unique stores and malls—those that offer a special appearance—as a surrogate or actual way to loosely interact with others. Only the most clinically depressed wished to stay at home forever. Most individuals crave human interaction, even in a community of "strangers" and thus, increasingly, shopping environments and products purchased by many people, became important amusement, entertainment, and social outlets.[5]

The original Niketown in Chicago is a veritable museum of popular culture and more accurately a temple to the fusion of sports, marketing, and television. Niketown is the definitive fusion of retail and entertainment.[6] On display in museum-like cases are shoes and clothing worn by famous athletes—all of whom are paid Nike endorsers. Hipper than most museums and certainly directly relevant to younger consumers, Niketown in Chicago and a host of Niketowns throughout North America appeal to the consumer as connoisseur of popular athletic culture in the same way that the Hard Rock Café appeals to the afficionado of Rock and Roll. Niketown's concept borrows heavily from many of the most successful department store appropriations of museum culture. What distinguishes the Niketown concept from the museum is the level of sophistication. Niketown is almost all about an "experiential" environment rather than a simple retail one. With its video clips constantly running or the elaborate displays, what is occurring is a form of theatrical entertainment presented upon a full-fledged retail stage.[7] Entering New York's Niketown is a "bedazzling" experience. One is overwhelmed, by the sights, sounds, lights, and displays. Although other retailers have caught up, for a time, there was nothing like going into one of these lifestyle entertainment environments.

The signature Niketown in Chicago attracted some 12, 000 people a day to the 69, 000-square-foot museum-like complex in the years since it first opened. It contained a basketball court, giant fish tanks filled with tropical fish, and of course, a host of sports memorabilia. At the time, this made the store one of the most popular tourist attractions in Chicago, surpassing the Lincoln Park Zoo and the famous Art Institute in visitor attendance.[8]

Niketown's attention to detail is legendary. Every corner and crevice has its own lighting and its own music. This experiential approach moves the shoes and satisfies in many ways. Thomas Hine relates how "delighted" some visitors are to discover "that the patterns on the manhole covers that decorate the floor allude to the waffle-patterned soles of the first Nikes."[9]

Niketown in London is divided into separate areas devoted to specific sports, but all converge on a central point or "town square" where most of the new launches and information activities are announced from the stage. There are photos of athletes playing sports displayed through a three story, 360-degree multimedia projection process. Museum-like exhibits detail the technology that has been developed for producing sports attire.[10]

Niketown is at the forefront of engaging consumers in an all-encompassing entertainment experience. Nike Park in Paris takes this a step further by encouraging visitors to literally enter into the sports experience. They can participate in numerous interactive stations, play football on a reduced-scale field and in general engage in the most exciting aspects of the game.[11]

In the New York store, Nike has utilized virtually every visual, traditional, and technological component to create an experience that rivals what can be seen on 42nd Street. Upon entering the store, the customer goes through turnstiles, as one would at a sporting event. A massive video screen plays a hip program, which showcases the company's products. One can interact with a variety of props, such as a punching bag, which harkens back to more retro feelings or simply be dazzled by the sophisticated "theme park" experience.[12] The Chicago Niketown has also been characterized as a supreme example of "retail theater."[13]

Where Niketown began, other retailers have attempted to capitalize on the appeal of consumer interaction or go in even bolder directions. At the Oshman's Supersports stores, size is key. According to a description of the Auburn, Washington, store, "The 85,000-square-foot space is pure entertainment." Not only is there the now-common putting green, but there is also an archery range, a batting cage and regulation and miniature basketball courts.[14] At The North Face in Chicago, there is a climbing wall, and a variety of ground surfaces in an area where customers can set up tents or lie on sleeping bags to get a more exacting feel.[15]

One of the most innovative of the e-stores has been the creation of American Girl Place department stores in New York and in Chicago. These stores literally create an entire mythology of the upscale doll and then create a self-contained environment devoted to the doll and its culture. Inside the merging of the retail and entertainment environment is seamless. There is a "theater and an original musical revue, a café, shops, a bookstore, a salon, and a variety of events and programs designed to bring the dolls and their stories even more alive for the visitors." Girls and their mothers or guardians can partake in a wide array of activities from having their photo taken to cooking classes. Like Walt Disney World it is crowded and stimulating, creating a loyalty and attraction that is remarkable.[16] It has become a definitive example of retail merged with entertainment. Girls can take in a show, which tells the story of one of the dolls. There are books on a wide array of subjects devoted to girl culture as well as dioramas, which focus on historical periods. It is like walking into a world completely apart from the everyday.[17]

The opportunity to try something, to actually test-drive a product, has great appeal to the prospective purchaser. This hands-on ability pulls together shopping, entertainment, and leisure in a unique way. During the cold winter months in Toronto, it is not uncommon to see avid golfers putting on the artificial putting surface at Golf Town. Hours can be spent honing one's skill. At Mountain Equipment Co-op in Toronto, there is a climbing wall. People who are not necessarily buyers—let alone climbers—visit into the store alone, or with children, in order to climb the wall. At Ikea, the Swedish furniture power store, all nicely accented in

Sweden's national blue and yellow colors, one can drop off the children in a play area and browse the various parts of the store, have dinner, a coffee, and at a leisurely pace. In Seattle, Washington the REI or Recreation Equipment Incorporated store has thought of virtually everything: there is a "475-foot-long mountain-bike test track, a rain room in which to test waterproof clothing, a faux hiking trail on which to test boots, and a 65-foot-high indoor rock-climbing pinnacle."[18]

Cybersmith in White Plains, New York, has dozens of computer stations where prospective purchasers can try computer software, CD-ROMs, and computer games. To make the experience even more hands-on and entertaining, there are also "state-of-the-art 'virtual reality pods' and 'simulation stations'" as well as the ability to order food and drinks from an online cafe, directly from the station.[19]

For years, record and later tape and finally CD stores, such as HMV, have been at the forefront of making entertainment and shopping synergistic. Whether it is the lighting, the displays, or the loud music, it is often these mega-stores that are synonymous with the e-store concept. On a smaller scale than climbing walls, it was possible to listen to music at various stations strategically placed throughout the store. TV screens and monitors lent visual accompaniment to the aural, with their nonstop videos and flashy images. One may not have always purchased the CD there but one could be entertained. And like the Sony and Niketown phenomenon, after the experience of one of these stores, one would become much more brand familiar.[20]

The Bass Pro Shops Outdoor World store, which opened in November of 2004 north of Toronto, is a huge store with every conceivable opportunity to blend shopping into entertainment. This flagship store at a state-of-the-art mall contains a 24,000 gallon aquarium, a 10,000 gallon trout fishing stream, a NASCAR simulator and an interactive arcade. The mall itself utilizes all the bells and whistles of the e-store. At each of the entrances there are sculptures and within the mall itself there are themes reflecting the Province of Ontario's diverse regions. There is a bowling alley, Lucky Strike Lanes, which has an upscale, retro decor and excellent food. At the NASCAR SpeedPark, there are four racetracks for go-karts.[21] This extremely large mall and all its entertainment appendages, both within and on the periphery, is part of the move to fully integrate shopping as an entertainment experience. Yet retailers and developers are recognize that not everyone gravitates toward these entertainment spectacles. To some extent there is a backlash against this form of hyper entertainment, leaving some consumers to search for less intense forms of shopping as an entertainment experience.

Coffeeshops now sell us a host of products as well. One can enter a Starbucks or an independent cafe and see a variety of mugs and cups, coffee machines, grinders, and a variety of seasonal merchandise. Starbucks CDs sell extraordinarily well. The music playing over the sound system is always enticing and mood-enhancing.

Drinking coffee seems to be a hugely appealing feature for potential shoppers. Most of the book superstores now have coffee bars, lunch counters, not to mention a host of ancillary pseudo-educational activities designed to draw people in. Evenings with authors can be interpreted as simply publicity for the book, but one must concede that perhaps something deeper is at work.

Bookstores are among the most often-cited destinations for shopping as an entertainment experience. Books are often the antithesis of the e-store phenomenon. Yet, the bookstore ambience can be completely and overwhelmingly entertaining. It provides social interaction, intellectual stimulation, and a comforting sense of well-being. Children's areas in these stores can also appeal to what the e-store phenomenon is truly about. Play areas abound, as do climbing furniture, puppet show stands, and a host of similar features. The latest DVD is sure to be playing on a large, wafer-thin television, positioned to challenge the books in the children's area. One of the major attractions of the bookstore is author readings. In the past one may have had to go to a university or lecture hall, but now one can go to a bookstore and hear the latest author read from his or her work.

Over the past ten years the creation of shopping zones or districts further merge shopping with entertainment culture in myriad ways. These include a host of renovated "districts" that once housed factories and warehouses to full-fledged entertainment complexes that resemble movie sets. In Costa Mesa, California, both *The Lab* and *The Camp* take these entertainment experiences to extreme levels. Retailers are merged into the entertainment environment in novel and creative ways. Shoppers can try a wide variety of lifestyle products in complete freedom, such as surfboarding in a wave pool or skateboarding on ramps. These "shopping playgrounds" merge the retail with the entertainment.[22]

If one takes the cultural appeal of the bookstore and merges it with some of the entertainment enticements inherent in a mall, one could get a unique environment, such as has been created in San Francisco. Metreon is a merging of high-end retail with high-brow culture. Metreon mixes interesting and appealing museums and galleries with theaters and retail environments such as the Gap and Barnes & Noble. Other retailers include a flagship Discovery Channel Store and large-scale entertainment stores such as one based on Maurice Sendak's *Where the Wild Things Are*. The Sendak store will follow the famous story and come complete with games and possibly a restaurant. Even more ambitious is a store based on David Macaulay's *The Way Things Work* project, complete with interactive displays, large-scale mock-ups and 3-D video presentations.[23] The Sendak and Macaulay stores, along with the Discovery Channel shop, are considered to be cutting-edge as far as retail entertainment options. They harness the glamour and spectacle of electronics and merge it with the entertainment appeal of popular culture. The goods for sale are either familiar to adolescents and their parents or are enticing because of their setting. People are not just entertained in these places; very often they are excited. The overwhelming displays stimulate potential consumers and browsers.

A retail environment does not have to be extreme to become an entertainment experience. Certain manufacturers have created micro-settings that appeal, as entertainment, in very sophisticated and subtle ways. The Williams-Sonoma chain has perfected a "retail as theater" arrangement by holding cooking classes and product demonstrations complete with samples. And by utilizing descriptors and narratives to contextualize their products, the products are infused with a story, complete with "imagination and romance."[24] This is a very successful tactic that first attracts the customer to the environment, then stimulates him/her by the products until the customer is comfortable in the entertainment, retail realm. It works on a low-key level yet retains enormous potency. According to two management consultants, this works extremely well in smaller, less "hyper" entertainment environments. The focus is on "sophistication and discernment." People are curious and interested and will eventually buy something. The creator of the chain uses a narrative structure to great effect. "Almost every product in the store is presented with a sense of place, history, culture, or adventure."[25]

Theme restaurants such as Planet Hollywood and the Hard Rock Café, entertainment stores such as the Disney Store or The Warner Bros. Store, fuse entertainment with consumption in a potent way. According to marketing guru Paco Underhill, "From a child's perspective, these places are like amusement parks that just happen to sell merchandise."[26] They become synonymous with fun and excitement.

But more can be at work within such extreme shopping/entertainment environments. Whether Bass Outdoor World, Niketown, or the ESPN Zone, something unique is at work. In a seminal article on these environments, John F. Sherry Jr. begins by piecing together some of the elements of their appeal. Sitting in the overdone Fox Sports Skybox sports bar in the Chicago airport, he is provoked to wonder about his attraction to these type of places. Sherry writes,

> The Skybox is a dense metaphor, playing off its literal emplacement in an airport, its passing resemblance to the luxurious glass palaces perched atop arenas and stadiums, and the surround of television monitors engulfing its patrons. I'm boxed in on a number of levels, packaged effectively as part of a consumption spectacle.[27]

The spectacle vacillates between hi-tech and nostalgia, the themed future and the manufactured past. Like the process of syncretic formation, Sherry feels that sports-oriented cultural constructions in particular "hybridize" and select. They merge the "high and low" with the "exotic and familiar"; they incorporate the outdoor with the indoor. "Inside these stores," he writes, "I can climb rocks, rappel, shoot weapons, fish and paddle, and toss and kick balls; virtually, I can skydive, race motorcycles and stockcars, golf, and bowl."[28] At the ESPN Zone, the area where the video and other games are situated is called the Arena. As Sherry relates,

> The Arena is reminiscent both of an arcade and of a carnival midway; the miniature courts, rinks, alleys, fields, and tracks enshrined within its ersatz stadium give something of a *wunderkammer* feel to the area as well. Ubiquitous television monitors apprize the patrons of the progress of contests in a host of sports around the globe, punctuating the flow of flaneurs around the space. Hyperstimulation and sensory overload are the order of the day, the feeling of being overwhelmed dominating the experience of most visitors.[29]

This over-sensitization is the appeal of the place. It is everywhere and it is overwhelming. In environs such as ESPN Zone, there are a variety of alternatives, which vary in their visual and almost kinetic appeal. From the "throne zone" with its leather recliners to the eating area complete with all the trappings of sports memorabilia, a visual melange of sights is designed to overwhelm.

It is not always necessary for shopping zones and entertainment environments to go to such extremes. Traditional, nostalgic fare is also appealing, as the bars and restaurants outfitted with faux artifacts and signs from the past can attest. The rise of "retro-shops" speaks to a shopping audience that wishes to purchase products of the past and engage in a world where jukeboxes, neon lights, and Zippo lighter displays reign supreme.[30] This appeal, which is something Ralph Lauren has tapped into, is harmonious with the postmodern attempts to conflate historical epochs. Another way of expressing why the retro is so appealing is that it is based on nostalgia rather than history. According to Christina Goulding, who incorporates the ideas of Fred Davis, nostalgia "is memory with the pain removed."[31] It puts a positive spin on feelings, which is one reason why certain toys and toy experiences are so potent to adults.

Like the Museum Store, the Past Times chain has created a venerable selection of retro "reproductions" in retro-styled stores. Located throughout Britain and Europe, this chain appeals to many versions of the past through its decor and its offerings. Little rooms or "interiors" are set up with representations of historical eras. A key attribute is the utilization of "display cases, pseudo-curatorial labeling and period music" which gives the shops and the rooms a museum-like appeal.[32] This highly successful concept will be explored in greater depth in chapter 7.

Even the more 'traditional' children's environments serve as entertainment outlets. The appeal of traditional toy stores seems unbounded. Many parents get excited upon seeing a display of toys, games, and stuffed animals that they may have played with when they were children. In turn, they react to this in a manner that is quite telling—at least to marketers. The nostalgic appeal of certain toys to parents is almost automatically imprinted on the children. This has been reworked on a very sophisticated level with the "toys" chosen, seemingly at random, by Restoration Hardware. Whether the traveling bingo games, classic cards, or wooden logs, the appeal is simple and grand. As accents to theme rooms or specific furniture displays, they reach out and grab the child within the adult. The larger toy chain has to work on a different level. Other forms of entertainment attraction supplant all the quaintness and nostalgia.

The Toys "R" Us chain has a number of entertainment offerings. At the flagship store in Times Square, there is an enormous "Ferris Wheel, a two-story Barbie dollhouse, a life-size version of the board game Candy Land complete with real candy (for sale)" as well as a number of sophisticated electronic offerings on very large screens.[33] It is a miniature version of Disney right in the middle of New York. But one does not have to be in New York to take advantage of shopping as an entertainment experience through Toys "R" Us. Anywhere on a rainy day, many parents roam the aisles of Toys "R" Us with their young children just for something to do. Children in the store are free to ride the bikes, test-drive the miniature electronic cars, or sample, and even break, a vast array of merchandise. Inevitably, the ideal for the merchant is to sell something and that is why this behavior is tolerated. As Ellen Seiter writes,

> Children may run and shout and cry and rip packages and drop merchandise, and it almost seems that no one is watching. For many mothers, Toys "R" Us is a place were children can be brought to kill time, to play on indoor equipment when the weather is too bad to go to a park. . . . Parents and children come "Just to look" as a form of entertainment in itself. . . . If Toys "R" Us is itself the entertainment, the cash registers are the place where the dramatic climax is reached.[34]

Even outside the store or just at its edge, purchases are still possible. These are comparable to some carnival giveaway. There are rows of toy dispensing machines that will cough up a trinket or a trifle for a dollar or two; a cheap way to get out of buying something expensive for the kids. And when the family is hungry, another version of the entertainment toy emporium exists.

Chuck E. Cheese, Dave & Busters, and other food emporiums serve as versions of entertainment shopping. In these spaces, one can play, eat, and redeem expensively acquired coupons for cheap merchandise, which can satisfy all the key desires.

The fact that "entertainment" culture has pervaded virtually every element of society suggests that shopping as an entertainment experience has become much more sophisticated and much more aware, from an industry point of view, of all that is necessary to constantly entertain potential shoppers. The definitive models of entertainment retailing are of course Gruen's malls and Disney's theme parks. From these starting points, which were much more sophisticated than Coney Island, the e-tainment version of shopping has matured and grown. What Disney pioneered had been perfected in a variety of environments.[35] What has occurred as a result of this evolution is that shoppers increasingly come to expect a store or retail environment to be stimulating and exciting. According to a report issued by the International Council of Shopping Centers, retailers and developers want to facilitate this experience, "because entertainment creates excitement and generates interest, it attracts people to shopping centers to shop and to do things besides shopping. More and more the shopping experience is becoming an entertaining lifestyle trend."[36] Very much related to this is the fact that shopping can provide appeal that stretches beyond acquisition. The ideas of satisfaction and desire are key motivators in the realm of shopping as an entertainment, even therapeutic, experience.

NOTES

1. Gary Cross, *An All-Consuming Century: Why Commercialism Won in Modern America* (New York: Columbia University Press, 2000), 184.

2. See David Nasaw, *Going Out: The Rise and Fall of Public Amusements* (New York: Basic Books, 1993), cited in Michael D. Beyard, et. al., *Developing Retail Entertainment Destinations*, Second Edition (Washington: Urban Land Institute, 2001), 4–7.

3. Beyard, et. al., *Developing Retail Entertainment Destinations*, 10.

4. Beyard, et. al., *Developing Retail Entertainment Destinations*, 10.

5. Russel W. Belk and Wendy Bryce, "Christmas Shopping Scenes: From Modern Miracle to Postmodern Mall," *International Journal of Research in Marketing* vol. 10 (1993), 289.

6. Donald Katz, *Just Do It: The Nike Spirit in the Corporate World* (New York: Random House, 1994), 82.

7. Joseph B. Pine II and James H. Gilmore, *The Experience Economy: Work Is Theatre and Every Business a Stage* (Boston: Harvard Business School Press, 1999), 63.

8. Donald Katz, *Just Do It*, 11.

9. Thomas Hine, *I Want That! How We All Became Shoppers* (New York: Harper-Collins, 2002) 199.

10. Otto Riewoldt, "Staging Brands," in *Brandscaping: Worlds of Experience in Retail Design*, ed. Otto Riewoldt (Berlin: Birkhauser Publishers, 2002), 22–23.

11. Riewoldt, "Staging Brands," in *Brandscaping*, 15.

12. Paul Goldberger, "The Store Strikes Back," *The New York Times* (April 6, 1997), section 6, 45ff, cited in George Ritzer, *Enchanting a Disenchanted World*, Second Edition (Thousand Oaks, Calif.: Pine Forge, 2005), 98, 99.

13. John F. Sherry Jr., "The Soul of the Company Store: Niketown Chicago and the Emplaced Brandscape," in *Servicescapes: The Concept of Place in Contemporary Markets*, ed. John F. Sherry Jr. (Chicago: NTC Business Books, 1998), 110.

14. Martin M. Pegler, *Lifestyle Stores* (New York: PBC, 1996), 110.

15. Pegler, *Lifestyle Stores*, 134.

16. Michael J. Silverstein and Neil Fiske, *Trading Up: The New American Luxury* (New York: Portfolio/Penguin, 2003), 141.

17. Marianne Wilson, "American Girl Has Charm," *Chain Store Age* 75, no. 1 (January, 1999) 136–38.

18. Beyard, et. al., *Developing Retail Entertainment Destinations*, 19.

19. Martin M. Pegler, *Lifestyle Stores*, 138.

20. Donald Shillingburg, "Entertainment Drives Retail," *Architectural Record* (August 1994), 84.

21. See "Shopping," Section L, *Toronto Star* (Saturday, October 30, 2004).

22. Pamela Klaffke, *Spree: A Cultural History of Shopping* (Vancouver: Arsenal Pulp Press, 2003), 52–55.

23. Mary Beth Knight, "Shopping with Class," *Chain Store Age* 75, no. 4 (April 1999), 79–80.

24. Michael J. Silverstein and Neil Fiske, *Trading Up: The New American Luxury*, 164–65.

25. Silverstein and Fiske, *Trading Up*, 164.

26. Paco Underhill, *Why We Buy: The Science of Shopping* (New York: Simon and Schuster, 1999), 149.

27. John F. Sherry Jr., "Bespectacled and Bespoken: Gazing from Throne Zone to Five O'Clock and Head," in *Time, Space, and the Market: Retroscapes Rising*, eds. Stephen Brown and John F. Sherry Jr. (Armonk, N.Y.: M.E. Sharpe, 2003), 22.

28. Sherry Jr., "Bespectacled and Bespoken," 22.

29. Sherry Jr., "Bespectacled and Bespoken," 23.

30. Christina Goulding, "Corsets, Silk Stockings, and Evening Suits: Retro Shops and Retro Junkies," in *Time, Space, and the Market: Retroscapes Rising*, eds. Stephen Brown and John F. Sherry Jr. (Armonk, N.Y.: M.E. Sharpe, 2003), 64.

31. Goulding, "Corsets, Silk Stockings, and Evening Suits," 65.

32. Stephen Brown, "Retro-Marketing: Yesterday's Tomorrow's Today!" *Marketing Intelligence & Planning* 17, no. 7 (1999), 364.

33. George Ritzer, *Enchanting A Disenchanted World*, Second Edition (Thousand Oaks: Pine Forge/Sage, 2005), 99.

34. Ellen Seiter, *Sold Separately: Parents & Children in Consumer Culture* (New Brunswick, N.J.: Rutgers University Press, 1993), 210.

35. James J. Farrell, *One Nation Under Goods: Malls and the Seductions of American Shopping* (Washington: Smithsonian, 2003), 164–65.

36. Cited in Farrell, *One Nation Under Goods*, 175.

6

Shopping As
Entertainment Therapy

Studies have shown that the notion of "desire" is a very significant aspect of the realm of consumption. Specifically, the idea of desire occupies a central place, which can straddle both the world of seeing and the world of buying. Intimately related to this are things such as fantasy and imagination, which in turn give rise to very vivid cravings. One woman in her late thirties, an academic with stellar political credentials, admitted that wherever she goes she seems to be looking for things to buy. After visiting a new urban renewal project in downtown Toronto, she felt disappointed that there was nothing yet available to purchase. Although there were galleries and restaurants, no shops had opened. Visiting this environment did not fully satisfy her because nothing was available for purchase. Many individuals have become so acclimatized to shopping in virtually any environment or space—at the very minimum, having the ability or freedom to look at objects for sale—that without this option, they are left unsatisfied.

For some people, shopping is *the* most exciting experience they engage in. Nothing else even comes close. It is comforting, pleasing, and stimulating. Whether it is the ability to handle beautiful and luxurious goods or the fantasy element of where those goods will take you, shopping can be intoxicating.[1] Even going inside a retail venue has ramifications. When one enters a well-appointed department store or an elaborately set-up shopping mall, the elements of consumer culture, natural desire, and Western material yearning seem to coalesce and kick into overdrive. As one respondent stated, "It is the only time that I feel truly excited. Nothing else does it for me!" Shopping environments are all-encompassing in this sense. In her research for the American chain Target, Laura Rowley found that this unique store seems to pull people in, in a way that the customers found hard to resist. Rowley writes:

> Almost everyone I interviewed for this book told me they have an inchoate longing to go there. They feel good roaming the aisles of the discounter but can't explain why.[2]

According to Rowley, customers feel good inside Target. They seemingly wish to be there, to wander and explore, and to unwind. The attention to detail seems to appeal to the customers, as does the fresh and clean look. This is in contrast to the darkness and dinginess of many large discounters. The warehouse look is somewhat insulting to sophisticated shoppers. They want to stay and browse and accordingly are invited to.[3] Rowley cites one customer, who after numerous poor shopping and service encounters, goes into Target and suddenly, is transformed and feels better. He went so far as to suggest that "when you go into Target you think, 'Yeah, maybe this is the perfect world. It's like the sun shines. Things are orderly, they're where they're supposed to be, people want to help you, they're friendly to you.'"[4]

Colin Campbell, in his seminal work on the correlation between the romantic ethic and modern consumption, suggests that looking at the many products offered for sale is an intensely stimulating exercise. It sparks fantasy and serves as a catalyst for the creation of daydreams. In certain respects, this "illusory enjoyment" is intensely personal and reflects and complements individual desire. At the same time, many people can experience the same heart-felt wants and needs and thus can participate in an approximate, "parallel experience."[5] Campbell argues that these "universal daydreams" provide insights into people's desires to crave the same things:

> . . . recognition of the importance and universality of day-dreaming helps to account for that basic taste for novelty which is shared by all modern consumers, and hence also for the existence of that most central of all institutions of modern consumerism—the phenomenon of fashion.[6]

There is, on the one hand, a universal sense of want and desire, as well as an almost individual-based communal appreciation of attraction to goods. In many cases we all want the same things, but different versions and for different reasons. So powerful is this that we need to have a tangible reminder of this yen.

In doing some research before a trip to France, I was searching a large national bookstore's Web site for titles on the history of France and in particular, Paris. What popped up in significant quantity were books on where to shop and how to shop. The increasing conflation of travel with shopping was only too evident in the search. Numerous books, at least a dozen out of the first twenty titles, reflect this passion. Wandering around Paris, one sees why this category of publishing is so successful. Tourists love to shop. Everyone, regardless of their budget, must buy something, no matter how tacky or inexpensive. Rather then spend time in museums or cultural sites, it seems that people want to shop. At the very least, on a trip, what they want to do is peruse the stores. In one instance, a respondent to the question about travel and shopping wrote that she was going to China for four days—just to shop! The desire to buy when away merges into how we think of ourselves. It is no longer enough to state that one has been there or to show a photograph, one has to produce an item that they purchased at the silk market or a quaint little store in Montmartre.

Research on tourism and the acquisition of artifacts or souvenirs, suggests that this important action within the confines of being away, becomes a touchstone when memories of places visited are recalled.[7] Just as important is the giving of a gift, especially one that has been purchased in a special place, and one not readily available at home. These two justifications for shopping while on a trip speak volumes about the relationship between shopping and entertainment. And this is not something new. Whether on a grand tour or sleeping on the beach in Goa, people always brought things back—for themselves, as totems or mementos or as gestures for those they thought about.[8] What is new today, and what has been discussed in this work, is the fact that shopping is a key motivator in tourism today. By key the suggestion is not that a few things are picked up while browsing, but literally, the main reason why people may go to a specific destination.[9]

The rise of "Lifestyle" shopping as a category, which touches on every aspect of one's life, is a key answer to the fact that shopping is seen as vital. By "Lifestyle" what is being referred to is the whole enchilada; it is about the way we live or the way we perceive ourselves to live. What we choose to wear or do, eat or see, is based on and related to our image or how we perceive ourselves or how we wish others to see ourselves. According to one authority, at its core, "lifestyle shopping is an egocentric experience, because you shop for the inner self—the real you." The example given is someone who goes on a golf vacation, but spends an inordinate amount of time dressing like a golfer and shopping for golf products. This golf mentality affects the shopper and comes to define him or her. Every purchase, accordingly, puts "your dream into virtual reality." What this could mean is that "the very act of shopping has become a lifestyle."[10]

Entering certain stores that speak to one's passions, hobbies, or desires, allows a consumer to obtain an object that symbolizes what they wish to be thought of or want to be—or even, what they literally are. Buying the product and taking it home is only part of the process; carrying the bag it is in is even more important to some. The excitement is in the package, and accordingly, opening it is "ultimately a drama, and its unwrapping has a particular psychology."[11] This rekindles memories of opening a Christmas present or of receiving a well-wrapped and beautifully presented gift.

According to research findings, many people have dreamt about things that they do not own but which they look forward to buying.[12] This speaks volumes about the place of shopping in contemporary culture. Most critics seem to feel that the desire to consume is put in place by the massive marketing and advertising culture that literally surrounds us like some layer of invisible gas. It is felt that this ubiquitous force co-opts people into purchasing. To some extent, one would have to agree with this conclusion. But what about before there was mass advertising? Or what about cultures that do not have access to advertising? Is there some inveterate desire to acquire things?[13] Historically, the answer would be yes. Individuals have always coveted items and things beyond the prosaic. The notion of shopping only accelerates this idea.

The construction of retail environments as entertaining and stimulating enhances the ethereal appeal that they may have upon consumers. From the dream worlds of the department stores to the dreamscapes of the latest entertainment-oriented mall to the micro-worlds constructed by Ralph Lauren, there is always something to inspire the consumer. Store designers and marketers know that there are as many retail environments as there are dreams:

> Effective retail store design evokes a particular consumption dream-world for a consumer, whether it is the deliberately cluttered bins of sale merchandise in a department store basement that animate some customers to dig hands-on in hopes of unearthing a possible hidden bargain or the deliberately sparse boutique displays of high-priced sweaters exhibited in museum–like glass cases that animate some customers to experience the rarity, high price, and desirability of each item. Consumers choose whether the dreamworld presented in the retail space fits their current fantasies or their worst nightmares.[14]

According to James B. Twitchell, this is in fact why the early shopping emporiums were linked to dreams and were called 'places of enchantment.' Twitchell feels that one moves into an escape mode when one enters a mall. The mall has become an environment that can stimulate the shopper in many ways. It can entice and excite or it can calm and soothe. Citing Ira Zepp, Twitchell suggests that the familiar use of fountains and flowing water pacify and soothe the tired shopper, rejuvenating them when they are fatigued and refreshing them for more shopping.[15]

Many people find it invigorating to go shopping. Just as it is uplifting to see a certain movie and for many, inspiring to walk through a particular park, many people experience the same emotional states by going shopping. It is no secret that people acknowledge that shopping is a "stress buster" and that the ritual of going out to a favorite store and purchasing something new is a very common way of getting out of a funk. Shopping, for many, brings about sensations that run the gamut from arousal to perceived freedom, as well as fantasy fulfillment. One design authority deliberately seeks to use shopping and consumption as a way to enhance the everyday experiences of most people. His intention is to do away with pretension and to inject the shopping environment with artifacts and a presence that stimulate happiness and rekindle magic.[16]

Some people experience a kind of giddy euphoria upon entering a certain shop or going into the mall. They are enamored with the products on display and for sale in a way that everyday life does not inspire.[17] The individuals who study shoppers are the first to both recognize and admit that shopping fulfills some very key psychological mechanisms. For many people, especially for women, shopping is a "transforming experience, a method of becoming a newer, or perhaps even slightly improved person."[18] For some it is the bargain they are able to obtain after the leisured quest. After perusing Target and other discount retailers, the "psychological high" of buying something for a fraction of the cost that it is available elsewhere, is significant for some.[19]

Once individuals—again, women in particular—were made to realize or were convinced that it was okay to buy, a new kind of association was created. The first department stores served as a key transmission point in perpetuating the ideology of consumption by teaching women that not only was it acceptable to spend money but as well, and more vital, that spending money was a way to enhance both "psychic well-being and social standing."[20] For many people, shopping extends well beyond the bounds of normal activity and comes to stand for a multitude of experiences. In the following interesting passage, novelist Paul Auster describes his mother's equating of shopping with "self-expression":

> My father was tight; my mother was extravagant. She spent; he didn't. The memory of poverty had not loosened its hold on his spirit, and even though his circumstances had changed, he could never quite bring himself to believe it. She, on the other hand, took great pleasure in those circumstances. She enjoyed the rituals of consumerism, and like so many Americans before her and since, she cultivated shopping as a means of self-expression, at times raising it to the level of an art form. To enter a store was to engage in an alchemical process that imbued the cash register with magical, transformative properties. Inexpressive desires, intangible needs, and unarticulated longings all

passed through the money box and came out as real things, palpable objects you could hold in your hand.[21]

One reason for Paul Auster's mother deep gratification by the shopping experience could be that it does in fact fulfill a very key set of needs and desires. Jim Pooler likens this to Abraham Maslow's Hierarchy of Needs Pyramid in an adapted format. Pooler theorizes that in Mazlow's hierarchy we shop, in the most basic sense, in order to satisfy fundamental survival needs. As we move upward, security and belonging become part of the equation, and near the top, there is the key esteem component. Shopping for self-actualization is at the top and is, like esteem, an essential motivator. From the most basic to the most esoteric, the individual acquires more as he or she moves up.[22] It is important to bear in mind, that for many who indulge in shopping as a form of therapy, not all have to consume. Many people feel that simply seeing the items, or simply being in the store, is satisfying enough. Whether felt as provocation for dreaming or as a perpetual form of longing, many people are aware that to be tantalized is entertaining enough.[23]

Psychologist Mihaly Csikszentmihalyi suggests that going shopping has a very tangible 'end-result.' It is, for many, something to do. Given the forces affecting boredom and lethargy in contemporary Western culture, shopping is seen as an antidote to the fact that many people are not sure what to do with their leisure time. Going to a store or heading to a mall provides a focus. Significantly it is a "goal-directed activity," which "fills the experiential vacuum that leads to depression and despair."[24]

It is important to acknowledge that from a postmodern vantage point, with its focus on the hyperreality of spectacle, an abundance of choice and a wide array of possible shopping experiences, many people desire to peruse, to touch, and to frequent environments, and to interact with products that reference deeper meanings. On the one hand, this manifests itself in the search for more authentic products and experiences. This can take a number of forms. Questing for originality can be axiomatic in antique hunting, or looking at products that reflect an artisans touch. Frequenting shopping environments that have a nostalgic appeal are another way to satisfy this need. Traveling to places that are considered historical or heritage sites also falls into this category. In essence, for some shoppers/consumers, the search for authenticity or tradition links them to time when things, perhaps, were more "coherent and meaningful."[25]

What is important in this postmodern, spectacle approach to shopping, and what critics of consumption feel is extremely detrimental to the overall health and well-being of society, is the fact that shoppers move from place to place, mall to mall, store to store, in search of entertaining environments and in a quest not just for uniqueness and originality in products, but in virtually everything. This is motivated primarily by the surface appeal of shopping as an entertainment experience; the fact that we, as shoppers, are looking for stimulation and entertainment, manufactured fantasy, in order to continue being both satisfied and entertained. As Russell Belk and Wendy Bryce have commented, "rather than seekers of truth, we become hedonistic seekers of novelty and pleasure." Thus, the almost insatiable quest for products and materials, which temporarily alleviate boredom and vagueness. For many it becomes a quest, attempting to find fulfillment and satisfaction in the purchase.[26]

Once again, the Disney illustration is useful. Belk and Bryce cite Stephen Fjellman's work on Disney World in the above contexts. Significantly, Fjellman comments that in the alienated, postmodern environment, characterized by tantalizing images of luxury and created desire, shoppers may be driven toward purchases that define themselves as individuals rather than as members of a group.[27] Thus shopping is not only entertaining and amusing on a primal level, it has become something used to define and illustrate individuality in what some observers call an alienated society.

Changes in the evolution of social dynamics and the familial structure of the Western society have greatly altered patterns of consumption. Currently, what may define this evolution to one extreme is the fact that both parents/partners in a household work. Since that is often the case, shopping that can't be done during the confines of the workday has to be done in the evening, or better yet, on the weekend. Shopping going to the mall, Home Depot, Crate and Barrel, and other stores has become a key entertainment activity on the weekend.[28] Shopping becomes a very important way for families to engage in leisure time—together. As Thomas Hine has observed, the "drive to transform shopping into a form of family entertainment is in fact, an attempt to adapt shopping to contemporary living patterns."[29]

Many shoppers make it a point to visit specific shops on specific days or at specific times. The visits to these environments are a significant part of their leisure and recreation activities. "I'm usually at Sporting Life on the weekend, preferably Saturday morning. It is part of my routine, my path. I check out what's new and then head across the street to Roots. I visit some of the smaller stores and then head to Starbucks or the Second Cup."

As this work has repeatedly emphasized, shopping as an entertainment experience has more depth than one may first assume. It often marks key moments in our lives and certainly marks seasonal occurrences, from birthdays to Christmas. As Nathalie Atkinson puts it, "the passionate pursuit of consumer goods occupies a larger part of our lives and culture with every passing year. Shopping is one of the defining rituals of contemporary civilization."[30] Shopping-based activities dominate many people's social calendar. The spectacle of shopping, especially around Christmas time, is enchanting on many levels. Smells and sites merge with memories and activities to blur distinctions that once existed. Christmas has become an eagerly anticipated event on the calendar, with parties and shopping excursions, visits with Santa at the mall, and specific purchases—all part of the season. It is not solely about obtaining goods, but rather, it is intensely social, personal, and entertaining.

For so many people living in the West, freedom, and other essential value-based elements of life very often mean having the ability to shop for a wide array of consumer goods. It has even been noted that the Berlin Wall fell not because of political factors such as repression of fundamental freedoms, but because of the desire for the East Germans to have access to the consumer goods of the West.[31]

This can develop into a form of pathology where shopping as an entertainment or leisure activity means finding oneself in the form of objects. As with Paul Auster's mother, the fictional Billy Pilgrim, in Kurt Vonnegut's *Slaughter House Five*, also has a mother who finds herself in shopping. "Like so many Americans," writes Vonnegut, "she was trying to construct a life that made sense from things she found in gift shops."[32] This merging of personality to products has been termed, "the assembling of the commodity self."[33] According to Aaron Betsky, many individuals find their identities by "buying bits and pieces of consumer culture."[34] Retailers, developers, and shopkeepers realize what so many consumer critics seem oblivious toward. This is the fact that shopping is not simply the mere acquisition of goods. For many, shopping has become a way of life in the form of accepted leisure and entertainment. The storeowners and the mall barons are aware of this. People willingly go to the mall, want to go to the mall, and the mall now accommodates them. It is now possible to pay a fee and have access to a quasi-country club or member's lounge at the mall. The museum fatigue-like waves of exhaustion are now swept away in a tranquil oasis within the mall, where one can relax and recharge. These services and others, such as babysitting, workout facilities, and even internet hookups only accentuate the appeal of the mall or full-spectrum shopping environment.[35]

The bottom line for most retail establishments means getting people into the "store" with the hope that they will purchase *something*. This very simple equation has some very marketed results. Individuals who have the time or the means to frequent shopping environments are highly sought out. Those who have abundant breaks or are employed as shift workers or those who can make their own hours are often the prime targets for this approach. The concept of the "hospitality quotient" kicks in, in order to get people not just to come in but also to linger. It is particularly relevant to bookstores and other sophisticated retail environments. According to Tralee Pearce, "Retailers today are upping the hospitality quotient in the hopes that even more people will spend afternoons like mine, lingering a little longer and feeling a little more cultured in the process."[36]

The attraction of the shopping experience is so strong, that whole areas that were either once free of consumption possibilities or only marginally oriented toward them, have now embraced this notion. Most major airports and many minor airports are, if not mall-like in their shopping opportunities, close to getting there. In Milwaukee one can spend time perusing a first-rate used bookstore. In Toronto there are goods at the airport shops unobtainable in the city. And this does not include the major ports of entry at London or in Amsterdam. The Andy Warhol Museum in Pittsburgh and the Smithsonian in Washington, D.C., operate major retail outlets at their respective city's airports.[37]

For some, the attraction of shopping as a defining aspect of self-esteem crosses over into a dangerous arena. There is the suggestion that this correlation afflicts up to 8 percent of the American adult population, and has properties that are similar to obsessive-compulsive disorders.[38] Although shopping excites the senses and alleviates stresses, there is a pathology in too much dependence. Shopping, like other entertainment venues, is often used as a corrective to unclear or undefined longings. With compulsive shoppers, according to Donna Boundy, "the main (unconscious) purpose is using the stimulation and distraction of shopping, . . . to avoid unwanted feelings." Compulsive shoppers displace unpleasant feelings such as "depression, anger, fear, loneliness, or boredom" into the urge to shop. Shopping, as many know, alleviates these feelings and allows the shopper to feel a "sense of well-being, excitement, and control" while engaging in the act. It is afterward that the problems set in. Boundy feels that what often prompts this displacement is the "I deserve it" rationale. For compulsive shoppers, the spree is motivated by a "stress buildup and feelings of deprivation." Shopping becomes the panacea or "pseudopleausure" necessary to "compensate for feelings of unfullfillment or lack of awareness." The extremes that people will go to are quite startling in order to satisfy needs and fulfill longings. Bargain hunters are especially ruthless in pursuit of getting a deal; others amass enormous credit card debts; in any case the behaviors often mask deeper concerns. At issue here is often the fact that it is the thrill of the deal, rather than the object itself.[39] Yet this too has qualifications.

The relationship or common attributes of shopping as a form of a quest needs further commentary, as a result of the positive as well as the negative feelings generated. As anyone who has enjoyed roaming around a store or a mall in search of something unique or in search of a bargain can tell you, it is a very gratifying feeling. Finding the right thing or getting something special at a fantastic price is in fact part of the entertainment component. One person, who usually disdains all facets of shopping, has commented that getting a certain book at a very low price is enormously appealing. This is part of the hunt and the discovery. According to a designer of stores, "Part of shopping is discovering. It may even be a very important part of its appeal. It feels as though it is tapping into some primordial instinct we have for hunting or gathering—we like the actual process of finding things." He implies that all of our senses are heightened, that we, like hunters, scan our environment, taking in the impression of the place and what it has to offer. "That's the part of what makes shopping a fun thing to do. It is what distinguishes one store from another."[40]

At another extreme is the sense of euphoria experienced when shopping or when making the purchase. For some this can be as satisfying as virtually any other experience or sensation possible. It is not uncommon even for certain individuals to undergo a pronounced emotional response when making a purchase. In his novel, *I'll Take It*, Paul Rudnick describes the protagonist's emotional state during and after shopping:

> Joe loved shopping for clothes and had an addiction to costuming himself. Clothing was the most benign self-indulgence. Shopping for clothes felt like sex, with a comparable cycle of foreplay, orgasm, and afterglow. If Joe had smoked, he would always have languorously puffed a cigarette after hitting the menswear departments.[41]

Many individuals who define themselves by the goods that they possess are quite caught up in the intricacies of shopping. It is a very real undertaking, and one that provides them with an inordinate sense of well-being and accomplishment. From an early age, relates a man in his late forties, "I was conditioned to shop. My brother and I waited for the catalogues to arrive and we would go through them looking hungrily at the toys and electronics. Eaton's around Christmas time produced a very colorful book, one that we would look at for hours." This pleasant memory dovetails quite nicely with David Brooks's observation that shopping "is a form of daydreaming." Brooks suggests that walking and looking at merchandise in a store is a form of "dream kindling." Harmonious with the sense of self-creation that we often get from buying, Brooks writes that many of these daydreamers "are looking for things that inspire them to tell fantasy tales about themselves." What you do with a particular purchase, how you use it, brings pleasure to you and those around you. Very often though, he comments, the purchase is not as satisfying as the fantasy, nonetheless, they often "play along." Significantly, the notion of using shopping as a path toward pleasant daydreaming is for many people vital.[42]

Shopping unleashes numerous thought processes beyond fantasy and daydreams. As well, other characteristics and feelings are let loose in the process of frequenting malls and stores. Comfort is a key attribute that comes into being through shopping as an entertainment experience. Like watching one's favorite episode of a television show or rereading a book, frequenting certain stores has the ability to make a potential consumer feel at ease and relaxed. Having fun has also been recognized as being quite important in shopping as an entertainment experience. This point, referenced earlier in the chapter on the mall, focuses on a version of the pleasure principle. What this process leads to is immediate or "primary" responses and elements of gratification. To some extent, this is hedonistic in that this "type of consumption seeks fun, amusement, fantasy, arousal, sensory stimulation, and enjoyment."[43]

The powerful emotions excited in the consumer range from a desire to obtain satisfaction with being part of some series of associations to core empathic feelings stimulated by a sanitized version of the past. This last association arises in a significant way in home design stores that have sprinkled their environments with captive little rooms that look and smell perfect according to designers and marketers. A visit to Restoration Hardware for example, can reveal someone sitting in an overstuffed leather armchair in a corner, attempting to rekindle the complex feeling stimulated by the shopping environment. This is also why baked goods, certain perfumes and candles, specific forms of music, a selection of colors, and the use of lighting—when combined—prove to be intensely powerful. For many shoppers, this combines to trigger a sense of homey comfort that is actual or put in place by a Hollywood version of the hearth. According to Fred Davis the employment of domestic forms of nostalgia is so powerful because of its relation to the sentimental selective memories that one has to the "home" of one's childhood. Seen from the vantage point of an adult, one looks back to childhood in the home as a place of "warmth, security, and love." In fact an original definition of the concept of nostalgia suggests that there is a marked desire, a longing, to return to home.[44]

As well as these shopping environments making people exceedingly comfortable, they initiate a form of youthful vigor in potential customers. People may literally feel younger if they surround themselves with the products of their youth.[45] The adult boom in collecting toys is illustrative of this trend. The intensive participation in sports is also a symptom. In essence, anything that triggers a feeling of youth or a memory of growing up—whether a store designed in a retro way or a series of products that have grand youth appeal, comes to the fore as something desirable and pleasing for a certain segment of the population. And it becomes a very entertaining element in the process. One of the reasons certain advertisements employ nostalgia and retro symbolism, is because of this impact.

Barbara Stern suggests that the revival, on a seemingly constant basis, of packaging—lettering, bottle design, typography—that harkens back to the "past"—for cola or other products—is based on "the consumer's desire to mine his/her past for enjoyable memories that can be shared generationally."[46]

An interesting deviation to the above is the anthropologically based exploration into both gift giving and significantly, wrapping. Carefully packaging something in beautiful paper, and wrapping it up with attention evokes much more than an acquisition of goods. Within Japanese culture, the importance of wrapping a purchase or a gift is highly significant for a number of reasons. From giving the gift a sense of "cultural legitimacy" to extreme versions of "etiquette," the surrounding of a purchase with elegance and finery is suggestive of something more than crass materialism. On a macro level, the same could be said of the retail environment. What is unique in the Japanese context is that the purchase is transformed for consumption, to a form of spiritualism.[47] The design and architectonic properties of the SEED department store in Japan, extend this process. As anthropologist Millie Creighton has recognized, the SEED stores are oriented around "a journey toward creativity and personal development."[48]

As satisfying as shopping can be on a personal or psychological level, within the realm of entertainment and leisure, shopping also serves a highly social function for many people. It brings them together in certain places, allows them to interact, and even connect, in others. According to Sze Tsung Leong, "Few activities unite us as human beings in the way shopping does." Leong suggests that shops are so pervasive that it cannot be otherwise. In essence shopping so thoroughly pervades one's life that "by mere virtue of proportion, shopping has become inescapable."[49] This is not without its problems as Leong makes quite clear, but what also arises is the constant necessity for the machinations of the shopping universe to constantly change or retool in order to "keep up with the most subtle changes in society."[50]

It is vital to keep in mind that shopping is much more than the simple acquisition of goods. According to Jane Rendell, shopping "also has a symbolic function—goods represent social values." Consumers, according to Rendell, take a lot of pride in what they buy and they often identify, despite what Marx and many neo-Marxists imply, very closely with the implied status, lifestyle, or social identity that a certain good projects. There is even the feeling of delight that virtually everyone has experienced in some form, upon purchasing—even something as banal as a cup of coffee.[51] Some of these processes are highlighted in the following two chapters.

NOTES

1. Ann Satterthwaite, *Going Shopping: Consumer Choices and Community Consequences* (New Haven, Conn.: Yale University Press, 2001), 120.

2. Laura Rowley, *On Target: How the World's Hottest Retailer Hit a Bull's-Eye* (New Jersey: John Wiley and Sons, 2003), 2.

3. Rowley, *On Target*, 11.

4. Rowley, *On Target*, 67.

5. Colin Campbell, *The Romantic Ethic and the Spirit of Modern Consumption* (Oxford: Basil Blackwell, 1987), 92.

6. Campbell, *The Romantic Ethic and the Spirit of Modern Consumption*, 92–93.

7. See Beverly Gordon, "The Souvenir: Messenger of the Extraordinary," *Journal of Popular Culture* 20, no. 3 (1986) 135–46.

8. Dallen J. Timothy, *Shopping Tourism, Retailing and Leisure* (United Kingdom: Channel View, 2005), 76.

9. See Timothy, *Shopping Tourism, Retailing and Leisure*, chapters 3, 4.

10. Martin M. Pegler, *Lifestyle Stores* (New York: PBC/Rizzoli, 1996).

11. Cited in Millie Creighton, "The Seed of Creative Lifestyle Shopping: Wrapping Consumerism in Japanese Store Layouts," in *Servicescapes: The Concept of Place in Contemporary Markets*, ed. John F. Sherry Jr. (Chicago: NTC Business Books, 1998), 201.

12. Juliet Schor, *The Overspent American: Upscaling, Downshifting and the New Consumer* (New York: Basic Books, 1998), 70.

13. See Virginia Postrel, *The Substance of Style: How the Rise of Aesthetic Value is Remaking Commerce, Culture and Consciousness* (New York: HarperCollins, 2003), ix, x. The author cites Anna Quindlen discussing the fall of the Taliban and the move by citizens in Afghanistan to consume, almost immediately. The significant point regarding consumption and publicity is made in the following: ". . . liberated Kabul had no ubiquitous advertising or elaborate marketing campaigns." How then to explain this rampant consumerism? One answer could be, as the author writes, that "maybe our relation to aesthetic value is too fundamental to be explained by our commercial mind control."

14. Melanie Wallendorf, Joan Lindsey-Mullikin, and Ron Pimentel, "Gorilla Marketing: Customer Animation and Regional Embeddedness of a Toy Store Servicescape," in *Servicescapes: The Concept of Place in Contemporary Markets*, John F. Sherry Jr. (Chicago: NTC Business Books, 1998), 154.

15. James B. Twitchell, *Lead Us Into Temptation: The Triumph of American Materialism* (New York: Columbia University Press, 1999), 243, 244. In another of James B. Twitchell's books, *Living It Up: Our Love Affair With Luxury* (New York: Columbia University Press, 2002), Twitchell, 186, writes, that upon visiting Ralph Lauren's signature store on Madison Avenue, he himself experienced a very unique set of emotions: ". . . I was moving my hands through the *thick* silk ties in a display box. I was just turning them over while looking at all the terrible bric-a-brac on the walls. . . . This stuff, this terrible over-priced stuff, this stuff with that little dreadful polo pony on the fat end of the tie, was making me feel . . . what? Fantastic and a little sad, and in a moment I realized—I *really* wanted one of them."

16. Philippe Starck, cited in Rowley, *On Target*, 37.

17. Twitchell, *Lead Us Into Temptation*, 244.

18. Paco Underhill, *Why We Buy: The Science of Shopping* (New York: Simon and Schuster, 1999), 116, 117.

19. Rowley, *On Target*, 45.

20. Susan Porter Benson, *Counter Cultures: Saleswomen, Managers, and Customers in American Department Stores, 1890–1940* (Urbana: University of Illinois Press, 1988), 3.

21. Paul Auster, *Hand to Mouth: A Chronicle of Early Failure* (New York: Henry Holt, 1997), 7.

22. Jim Pooler, *Why We Shop: Emotional Rewards and Retail Strategies* (Westport, Conn.: Praeger, 2003), 139–54.

23. Campbell, *The Romantic Ethic and the Spirit of Modern Consumption*, 92–95.

24. Mihaly Csikszenmihalyi, "The Costs and Benefits of Consuming," *Journal of Consumer Research* (September 2000), 270.

25. Russel W. Belk and Wendy Bryce, "Christmas Shopping Scenes: From Modern Miracle to Postmodern Mall," *International Journal of Research in Marketing*, 10 (1993), 279.

26. Belk and Bryce, "Christmas Shopping Scenes," 279.

27. Stephen Fjellman, *Vinyl Leaves*, 1992, 38, cited in Belk and Bryce, "Christmas Shopping Scenes," 280.

28. Paco Underhill, *Why We Buy: The Science of Shopping*, 141, 142.

29. Thomas Hine, *I Want That! How We All Become Shoppers* (New York: HarperCollins, 2002), 189–90.

30. Nathalie Atkinson, "Retail Ritual," *The National Post* (Saturday, November 22, 2003), SP1. 143. See David Halberstram, *The Next Century* (New York: Random House, 1993), 1–20.

31. Kurt Vonnegut, *Slaughterhouse 5*, cited in Paul Fussel, *Class: A Guide Through the American Status System* (New York: Touchstone/Simon and Schuster, 1983), 127.

32. Stuart Ewen, *All Consuming Images* (New York: Basic Books, 1988), 79.

33. Aaron Betsky, "All the World's a Store: The Spaces of Shopping," in *Brand.new*, ed. Jane Pavitt (Princeton: Princeton University Press, 2000), 110.

34. See Anne Marie Owens, "The Best Kind of Retail Therapy," *The National Post* (Saturday May 26, 2001), W120.

35. Tralee Pearce, "Hospitality Retail," *The Globe and Mail* (Saturday, September 18, 2004), L1.

36. Karen Von Hahn, "Museum Stores," *The Globe and Mail* (Saturday, November 1, 2003), L3.

37. Michelle Lee, *Fashion Victim: Our Love-Hate Relationship with Dressing, Shopping and the Cost of Style* (New York: Broadway Books, 2003), 58.

38. Donna Boundy, "When Money Is the Drug," in *I Shop, Therefore I Am: Compulsive Buying and The Search for Self*, ed. April Lane Benson (Northvale, N.J.: Jason Aronson Inc., 2000), 7–8.

39. Cited in Paco Underhill, *Call of the Mall* (New York: Simon & Schuster, 2004), 176.

40. Paul Rudnick, *I'll Take It!* (New York: Ballantine Books, 1989), 21.

41. David Brooks, *On Paradise Drive* (New York: Simon & Schuster, 2004), 209–211.

42. Morris B. Holbrook and Elizabeth C. Hirschman, "The Experiential Aspects of Consumption: Consumer Fantasies, Feelings, and Fun," *Journal of Consumer Research*, vol. 9, (September 1982), 135.

43. Fred Davis, cited in Barbara B. Stern, "Historical and Personal Nostalgia in Advertising Text: The *Fin de siecle* Effect," *Journal of Advertising* 21, no. 4 (December 1992), 16.

44. Cited in Barbara B. Stern, "Historical and Personal Nostalgia in Advertising Text: The *Fin de siecle* Effect," 17.

45. Barbara B. Stern, "Historical and Personal Nostalgia in Advertising Text: The *Fin de siecle* Effect," 17.

46. Millie Creighton, "The Seed of Creative Lifestyle Shopping: Wrapping Consumerism in Japanese Store Layouts," in *Servicescapes: The Concept of Place in Contemporary Markets*, Ed. John F. Sherry Jr., (Chicago: NTC Business Books, 1998), 199, 200.

47. Millie Creighton, "The Seed of Creative Lifestyle Shopping: Wrapping Consumerism in Japanese Store Layouts," 202.

48. Sze Tsung Leong, ". . . And Then There Was Shopping," in *Harvard Design School Guide to Shopping, Project On The City 2*, directed by Rem Koolhaas (Koln: Taschen, 2001), 130.

49. Tsung Leong, ". . . And Then There Was Shopping," 131.

50. Jane Rendell, "Between Architecture, Fashion and Identity," *Architectural Design: Fashion and Architecture* 70, no. 6 (December 2000), 10.

51. Rendell, 10.

7

✛

Shopping As an Edu-tainment Experience—Dressing History: The Domain of Lauren

It is no secret that institutions of higher education of all sorts have moved toward models and modes of operation that have been influenced by consumer culture. Whether this means simply seeing students as customers, or merchandising and branding every aspect of their institution, market forces have invaded. But, is it possible for the reverse to hold true? Is there something within the worlds of retail and the universe of shopping that can in some way or form instruct or at least edu-tain? If other products of popular culture and mass-mediated culture can be employed to provide information, why not the combined worlds of clothing, fashion, and publicity? Advertising and marketing have employed pseudo-educational techniques to get people to use their products and have thus served to instruct millions. But the impact in teaching men to use a Gillete razor or to buy packaged goods[1] or to instruct women how to use a new cosmetic product is more blatant than the subtle forms of traditional educational offerings that can be proffered from the mass market. One sophisticated possibility is from the domain of Ralph Lauren.

In the post-modern universe, and one could argue, the modern one as well, there has been an increasing move toward a merging or blending of historical epochs. One could argue that this is the result of a television and now an Internet culture dictating the pace and the non-linear nature of contemporary society. To some this is a worry. To others, it doesn't matter. Chronological placement isn't as important as getting the message out. One manifestation of this in Daniel Bell's idea of "syncretism." Bell's view suggests that there is a mixing-up and merging of historical periods and that in realms of expression such as art, design, and architecture there are no longer any boundaries. Any element of what defines modernity is free to borrow and appropriate, which means that the return product or the end element, be it a sculpture or collage, a furniture manufacturers conception of the past or a clothing line, can take whatever its designers desire in syncretic appropriation.[2]

Another important trend to recognize in the world of marketing and selling is the increased utilization of history and nostalgia in advertising, store design, and product design. Both these concepts employ the utilization of "the past" in attempting to create an ambience or an association that is transferred from the product onto the consumer. The import of the past is not something that has simply sprung to life in the past few years. It is a device that has been engaged in previous times and applied to a wide variety of media. Nostalgia differs from history in that it is intensely personal and predicated upon personal memory, especially positive or "utopian" recollections, idealized and cleaner than the complexities of true history.[3] Given the fact that we are only a few years into a new century and importantly, a new millennium, the potency of history is particularly pronounced. The visibility of properties of the past is quite obvious and permeates a wide array of discourses, products, and ventures.[4] One reason for this authority has to do with the "dominance" of the past at a time of great change. There is a tendency to look back with intensity, at certain times, in order to recapture or find something that may be missing. This backward glance toward a previous era, complete with its material culture, is comforting to many and provides forms of escapist satisfaction as well as emotional security to many. This is exactly why it is often employed in the realms of consumer culture. The consumer—or for that matter, the reader and the viewer—latches onto images and associations that harness or activate the power of the past and that in turn provide satisfaction, comfort, and awareness.[5]

One of the points made repeatedly in this work is that advertising, in conjunction with consumer culture, is not simply the conversion of an abstract ideal into a tangible desire to purchase. The old adage of manipulating the consumer as "a victim" doesn't hold up in the way that it once did. What is a valid assessment is the fact that advertisers harness the desires that consumers hold in great stock. At the same time, the consumer is involved, and often, at an intimate level, in defining his or her identity by embracing what the advertiser has created or what the marketer has established. In essence, the purchasing of specific styles of clothes allows an individual to define or redefine their identity, which according to some theorists is as important as choosing a profession.[6]

When looking at the advertisements for the products of designer Ralph Lauren—whether Polo, Polo Sport, or Purple Label[7]—the words that come to mind are nostalgia, taste, refinement, class, and old money. What the people behind the ads do (no doubt with Ralph Lauren's full consent) is attempt to harness the patina of age, with all that that entails, in order to create a series or "worlds" where time stands still. The Lauren universe and the advertisements which spearhead their awareness, involves re-defining historical icons and packaging them in a way that makes them accessible, whether one is talking about Native American themes or the East Coast Anglo-American ethos.[8]

These ads, and the related marketing programs are quite similar to Roland Marchand's description of the popular "social tableaux." Marc-hand comments that "reflections of society" advertisements were utilized in early magazine illustrations to link people to specific social settings. They relied on "scenes sufficiently stereotypical to bring immediate audi-ence recognition." The social tableau advertisements of the 1920s and the 1930s had, as Marchand notes, a tendency to focus on an upper-class at-mosphere with such prevalence that "a historian relying exclusively on their manifest evidence could only conclude that most Americans of that era enjoyed an exceedingly affluent and leisured mode of life."[9]

A key trope in this recipe is the perception that what is stylistically "classic," in sartorial and material terms, is automatically equated with the casual yet sophisticated taste of the upper classes. Veblen's notion of the "veneration of the archaic," which as Paul Fussel has demonstrated, "shows itself everywhere," is a concept that many people hold in high esteem, if not revere.[10] This ideal holds sway across many facets of the advertised worlds of Ralph Lauren. What this means, in essence, is that the whole notion of oldness, of time, of history, cannot only be tastefully packaged, but more importantly, can hold great appeal to many people hoping to catch a morsel of the finery. The idea of a specific, high-class look, or more accurately, what John Seabrook calls the "haberdasherical embodiement of an Anglo-American aristocrat" comes significantly from the products of mass culture.[11] Lauren and others have been influ-enced by a variety of film and popular depictions which reflect a specific and defined version of the mediated past. The motion picture images, such a significant staple of entertainment culture, merge into the staples of the clothing universe. These images have been resurrected periodi-cally and have appeared in their own film versions: from *The Great Gatsby* to *Annie Hall* to *Out of Africa*. Just as earlier films and stars Cary Grant and Noel Coward provided examples to Lauren as an influence, both personally and professionally, they have been resurrected and re-cycled for a newer audience. This process has been combined with new retail avenues which have brought a formerly hard-to-find look to the general public.

Exclusive menswear shops and upper-market department stores were once the private shopping outlets for a select and wealthy clientele. Those that are around today, such as Saks and Barney's, have broadened their appeal, which in turn, has allowed them to capture as large a market as possible. Where once there were only a few shops in a few select cities, catering to the upper end of the market, they now dot the landscape and can be found in virtually every city and in most department stores in boutique form. In the past, shopping in these exclusive stores used to be a form of elite education—an introduction to a quasi-restricted arena. This was akin to taking a grand tour of Europe, summering in some exclusive resort, or going to the right school. The stores were part and parcel of a complete education in refinement, manners, and style. They provided a specific kind of knowledge to a very select group of individuals.

Now, access to such a world, or at least the vestigial trappings of "good taste," can be purchased by virtually anyone. Certain retail establishments offer a canned version: a ready-made adaptation of elite Anglo culture, accessible and obtainable for the right price. These shops (such as Polo Ralph Lauren), their products and their image(s), now provide direct access to the material conditions of culture, affluence, and tradition, that used to only be accessible through birth, education, and travel.[12] The Lauren ethos provides a very sophisticated shortcut to a world that was once the privilege of the few, but that now can be bought, accessed, and displayed.

The large, glossy, and tasteful Ralph Lauren images that grace the pages of *The Sunday New York Times Magazine, The New Yorker, Esquire, GQ, Vogue* and so on, are often block ads that feature a narrative lifestyle. For the most part group portraits or isolated fragments are the dominant features. The portraits are usually composed of three or four men and women, girls and boys—dressed in Ralph Lauren finery. The fragments are either close-ups of beautiful faces or snapshots of accessories such as socks, shoes, and ties.

From the obvious Polo logo to the "undercoded" tie or belt with no discernable badge, the viewer and potential purchases of virtually any product from the Ralph Lauren universe is automatically a member of a manufactured identity club. No special signet ring, no embossed care, are necessary, for the wearing of Ralph Lauren is entry and proof in itself that one is now part of a unique universe. One has purchased the image of wealth, class, and "the good life." This is primarily what is conveyed by the marketer's imagination in the ads and in the created style of Ralph Lauren. By purchasing the shirt, the scent, or the shoes, one has entered the exclusivity of the highest levels of society—at least symbolically and vicariously.

The world that Ralph Lauren creates is based on exclusivity yet, at the same time, is meant to attract the masses. What most people who purchase the Lauren lines of clothing and home decor want, at the very least, the accoutrements of historically grounded symbols of class. Lauren's advertising and imagery is directed toward this longing. Commodities of all kinds, from cars to watches, have become vital in defining self-worth. Not possessing the right look can be detrimental to one's self-esteem, one's career, and one's love life.[13] Beyond this very potent appeal, Lauren's world is a form of fantasy fulfillment for many. It harkens back to a mythologized sense of history, to an era when time stands still. An advertisement that appeared in the *New Yorker* and in other magazines in 1998 solidifies this approach. Pictured in black and white is a stone mansion, a vintage automobile, art deco furnishings, and walking sticks with silver handles. There is an attempt within this and other ads to convey a sense of time-slowed down in an effort to recapture the unhurried and leisured world of the country gentleman. The images imply an individual who does not have to worry about rushing but has the power to slow down time, to stop it, to almost capture it.

In an ad campaign run in the mid 1980s, Ralph Lauren wrote in the text, "There is a way of living that has a certain grace and beauty. It is not a constant race for what is next, rather an appreciation of what has come before. There is a depth and quality of experience of what is truly meaningful. . . . This is the quality of life that I believe in."[14] This fragment says much about the ethos of the Lauren ideal. "What has come before," is a reference to history, to myth, to tradition. This anachronistic approach to style allows the Lauren empire to capitalize on diverse and deep associations with historical allusions. Designers, filmmakers, and other purveyors of taste have often looked to the past for inspiration and more significantly, for authority. The power of the past to bestow influence is unlike any other force in lending legitimacy and status to something, especially something new. Architects, planners, and politicians seeking to quickly legitimize a new site or even a new ideology, resort to the power of classicism or another proven epoch, to prop up the new with something timeless.

This is also why historical signifiers permeate the invented worlds of Ralph Lauren. The tactile appeal of crocodile or the lusciousness of cashmere are automatic references to old money, exclusivity and even landed aristocracy. Kennedy-esque home in the Cape Cod style, festive groups gathered on manicured laws to play sports or just lounge, and images of intact familial generations (complete with grandfather/scion and grandmother/clan matriarch) are themes that are evoked again and again. By wearing, displaying or purchasing some facet of the world of Ralph Lauren, one is demonstrating that one possesses "class" or more accurately, the disposable income to don these clothes. It is as if the polo, the button down, the tasseled loafers or the tweed jacket gives one a *pass* into a dream world of taste, manners, old money and refinement. From the golf photos to the picnics, from yachting to the antique cars, the shorthand implied is a level of status and taste that was once the preserve of the elite but that now can be available to anyone with the sense/cents to buy.

The kind of historical signification utilized in the marketing and the construction of the world of Ralph Lauren is similar to the kind of history projected in Hollywood films and, to some extent, in tourist attractions that run the gamut from Disney World to Old West shows, pioneer villages and Colonial Williamsburg. It is a distilled form of historical mythology that reflects the kind of popular archetypes that most people can readily understand, relate to, and immediately process.[15] As architectural historian Witold Rybczynki writes, Ralph Lauren's clothes, themes, and ideas:

> . . . are based on recognizable homegrown images: the western ranch, the prairie farm, the Newport mansion, the Ivy League college. The feeling of deja vu is intentional: Lauren is an orchestrator of images. Although his clothes are not faithful replicas of period dress, their appearance does reflect popular ideas about various romantic periods of American history. We have seen them all before, in paintings, in photographs, on television, and, especially, in films.[16]

The advertisements exude the intangible notions of privilege and refinement, exclusivity, and even high culture. The attempt is to transfix the potential consumer with these signs so that s/he will desire this form of mass exclusivity, exclusively. The intentionality is subtle, yet extraordinarily effective.

At his signature store in New York, in the Rhinelander Mansion, now known as the Polo Mansion, all of this coalesces. What has been created, or transformed, is a repository for the essence of Polo Ralph Lauren. The Mansion is the Polo universe, its centerpiece and captured image rolled into one place. It has become a tourist attraction and suggests that if you want to understand Polo, if you want to know about the past as defined by Ralph Lauren, come in and look. Like a museum it is stuffed with antiques from Waterford and Cartier, photographs and books, old luggage and etched glass.[17]

The key to all this is the almost tangible wish fulfillment that is harmonious with so much about consumption and marketing: the desire to belong. Whether it is the notion of belonging to a family or a "feel good" lifestyle, Lauren makes it accessible, and for many, fun and amusing as well. Unlike couture, this is not about distinction or exclusion, but about *inclusion*.[18] According to none other than Martha Stewart, "When people buy his products, it gives them the feeling of having class and stature. They're buying a piece of his world."[19] And, so much of it *is* for sale.

In one main sense, clothing—or fashion—affords the viewer/wearer/ purchaser status. This operates on both overt and subliminal levels. The purchase of a polo shirt becomes a surrogate (albeit a false one) for entry into a world of wealth, taste, and distinction. This has always been so—in particular, since the court life of the fourteenth century—and continues to be the case today. Fashion, like the driving of certain cars or the wearing of a particular wristwatch, provides a sartorial shorthand for what the wearer wishes to be or be thought of. As Alison Lurie observes, "to choose clothes, either in a store or at home, is to define and describe ourselves."[20] By merging a fantasy world of Gatsbian plenty into the mass tastes of consumers, Ralph Lauren—the man, the empire, and the ads—tantalizes and entices the consumer into an environment that is barred from most, yet is purchasable to a degree. If fashion is about making one "feel special," providing an opportunity for "play acting" and lifting individuals "into a world of luxury or pseudo-luxury, beyond work, drudgery, bills, and the humdrum everyday,"[21] then Lauren has succeeded.

So effectively is this accomplished that the consumer becomes caught up in a world of Veblian consumption. What this can mean is that simply having *just one* article is not enough. The lone polo shirt in the closet "hangs" in diametric contradiction to the rules of plenty. A form of addiction takes over and there is the unstated desire or even the overt intention for the consumer/viewer to purchase multiples and in quantity. This yearning for more than just one suggests that the more you have, the closer you can become to the idealized vision in the ads. And this is supplemented by the ambiance of the stores and the intentions implied within the cologne and perfume advertisements.

In the Polo and Ralph Lauren shops (both free-standing and within department stores) the atmosphere of luxury, of wealth and of finery, is portable and transportable. In essence then, you can take the Lauren world home. Not only can you wear it, and not only can you exude the scent of it, but you can *live* it. This complete environmental spectrum means that you can sleep on it (through Lauren label sheets), shower with it (through Lauren towels), stare at it (through Lauren paints and wallpaper)—literally surround yourself with the world that Ralph Lauren has created. It becomes more than a product, more than an act of consumption—it becomes a lifestyle. In her profile of Ralph Lauren, for upscale *Town & Country*, Pamela Fiori sums up this all-encompassing universe:

> Long before I ever met him, Ralph Lauren was a part of my life. For years, I had slept on his sheets, dried myself with his towels, worn his clothes, applied his mascara and given Polo shirts, ties and fragrances as gifts (always

gratefully received) to the male members of my family. And although I have yet to paint a room in one of his hues or cuddle up with a lion cub, as model Bridget Hall does in his Safari ads, I hope one day I will.[22]

Thus, by surrounding oneself with everything "RL," one can enter the world of the ads! This is a world that has stood still, one that is not affected by the vagaries of industrial civilizations. In these ads, as in the Ralph Lauren universe, there is no reference to the capriciousness of contemporary society. These worlds are both historical recreations and ahistorical reconfigurations. The ads, like the stores and the boutiques, are devoid of anything that is technological or even modern. There are no clock radios, computers, and stereos. As Witold Rybczynski has astutely recognized, "There are pipe racks and humidors in the bedrooms, but no cordless telephones, no televisions. . . . The mechanical paraphernalia of contemporary living has been put away, and replaced by brass-cornered gun boxes, silver bedside water carafes, and leather-bound books."[23] Perhaps this is suggestive of the idea that the people who inhabit this world have servants to do the mundane tasks. The fantasy is of "old world splendor" or the "English country house" where living well is an art and a career. Here, there are no distractions. The absence of technology reflects the focus on the past. This is a nostalgic fantasy world when there were no intrusions, and in particular, reinforces the "veneration of the archaic" as an idea.

Clothing has the unique ability to serve, in the worlds of Fred Davis, as a "visual metaphor for identity." Consequently, the significance of dress and appearance as Goffman and others have recognized should not be discounted as trivial. Like possessions, clothing not only allows us to manage our ambivalences, but at the same time, for many people, serves to codify and classify what we want people to think of us.[24] Relevant here is the fact that since people began to wear clothes, the more expensive and elaborate the dress, then generally, the higher one's status. The expense of clothing was just as key to decoding who one was, as much as the "look." It was important for one "not to dress above one's station" and "sumptuary laws" periodically governed what one could wear.[25] What is essential here is the fact that, historically, vast gulfs separated the classes yet as the same time one could simply tell by looking at the garment and the wearer, whether or not it was dear. But as Alison Lurie has found, beginning in the twentieth century, "counterfeit" (re)productions, synthetics, and modern manufacturing techniques became so advanced that it was now possible to reproduce the finery of the upper classes for virtually everyone, and at affordable prices. A veritable identity crisis erupted which blurred distinctions and mingled classes.[26] Lurie feels that a bold idea was necessary to reinvent the high-status garment:

It was realized that a high-status garment need not be recognizably better or more difficult to produce than other garments; it need only be recognizably more expensive. What was necessary was somehow to incorporate the price of each garment into the design. This was accomplished very simply: by moving the maker's name from its former modest inward retirement to a place of outward prominence.[27]

One of the most significant aspects of the Ralph Lauren universe is the clearly identifiable Polo logo on the left side of the shirt. This icon is enormously rich in communication and affords the wearer a remarkable degree of currency. Like the Lacoste alligator, the Polo pony logo is one of the most potent displays of pseudo-high-class decor. Like the greatest brands and Barthian signifiers, it says in an economic form that this, for example, is not just a button-down shirt. This logo was chosen as a deliberate way to channel "class" into retailing. It has been extraordinarily successful. The polo player logo "communicated an image of sophistication and financial success," notes[8] Jeffrey Tractenberg.[28] Further, he recognized that, "as a selling tool its value would prove inestimable." The utilization of the horse, or the polo pony is a direct reference to upper-class culture. As Michael Korda writes, regarding the horse, "In countless ways the horse signifies rank, class, money, and has done so from the very beginning of history. . . . The horse stood, among other things, for social superiority . . . Horsemanship was the common bonding factor between the upper classes of almost every civilized nation and culture."[29]

The Polo line, complete with the hugely successful and ubiquitous fragrance, is predicated on the notion of privilege and exclusivity. This in fact, has been the marketing strategy. Polo and Ralph Lauren connote "good breeding," old money and tradition.[30] Since the company's inception there has been an enormous devotion to the props and material trappings of what was assumed to be the sartorial accouterments of high culture—walking sticks, alligator luggage, and other dear props. As Terri Agins puts it, these items "went a long way to weave a spell around Ralph's rich man's look and stirred all kinds of longings in people, the dream that the upwardly mobile shared for prestige, wealth, and exotic adventure.[31] Agins calls the more extreme and expensive offerings (such as a $7,000 mahogany high boy with tartan-lined drawers)—both as props and products—Polo's "dream merchandise." These very key symbols served to connect both customers and voyeurs, to aristocrats who sailed in Newport and adventurers who took safaris in Kenya.[32]

New money as well as old flocked to the Lauren universe. Lauren's formula, that of appropriating the establishment look—the elite WASP wardrobe of rugby shirts and Sperry Top Siders, of mansions and summer houses—became so successful that even the British royal family adopted

Polo.[33] Polo, the sport, is, despite its appeal currently with the Hollywood set, a highly elitist sport that has traditionally, historically, been played only by the very wealthy. Perhaps the crowning sanction of legitimacy came when the Metropolitan Museum was looking for a sponsor for its exhibit, "Man and the Horse." The natural and obvious choice was Ralph Lauren's Polo.[34] This exhibition focused primarily on clothing worn by moneyed Americans such as the Rockefellers as well as by cowboys such as Buffalo Bill. It could be said that the lines between culture and commerce have been crossed in the sense that the Polo logo was quite visible at the exhibit[35] but what was key was the association of Polo and Ralph Lauren with the significant lineage of the horse. The horse itself can straddle both ends of the spectrum. It can be used in the traditional, elitist sense, as with the game polo, or it can be harnessed in the more democratic sense, as with Chaps and the Ralph Lauren focus on the western cowboy myth.

By cleverly reconstructing "little worlds" of luxury, accurate down to the cashmere throw and crystal letter opener, Lauren has been able to harness a version of history that has been the preserve of the privileged few. Now, owing to Lauren marketing techniques, one need not be a full-fledged blue blood, but someone capable of spending the money in desire.

This straddling is harmonious with the way Ralph Lauren has always appropriated real or mythologized historical tropes. Whether it is the New England "All-American" family, the rugged modern-day cowboy, the safari-like luxury or any other "era," the Ralph Lauren version of it is extremely appealing in a society that values a material culture created from myth. The idea of transforming these myths into versions of reality has caught on and become an extremely important tenet in creation and maintenance of shopping as an entertainment experience. What is in the store as far as merchandise is not as important as the environment in which it is displayed. The entertainment and appeal quality of the retail atmosphere enhances the shopping experience and encourages people to come. Whether it is a combination of retro-marketing or the projection of a lifestyle series of associations, it attracts customers and builds many associative relationships.

Upon entering the Ralph Lauren boutiques, or the stand-alone stores, the attention to detail is arresting. One can see that enormous time and effort have gone into the construction of the store, the fixtures, the furnishings, and the color choices. Everything is there for a reason; almost everything has its place. Certain areas are delineated for certain styles and specific looks. Rooms are distinguished by their ambience. In essence these "little worlds" resemble period rooms where everything can be purchased. The extension of this approach has numerous variations. One such aspect is increasingly found in the museum.

NOTES

1. See Susan Strasser, *Satisfaction Guaranteed: The Making of The American Mass Market* (New York: Pantheon, 1989), chap. 4.

2. Daniel Bell, *The Cultural Contradictions of Capitalism* (New York: Basic Books, 1976), 13–14.

3. See Fred Davis, *Yearning for Yesterday: A Sociology of Nostalgia* (New York: The Free Press, 1979).

4. See Mark Moss, *Towards The Visualization of the Past: History as Image* (Vancouver: University of British Columbia Press, Under Review), Introduction, chap. 1.

5. Barbara B. Stern, "Historical and Personal Nostalgia in Advertising Text: The *Fin de siecle* Effect," *Journal of Advertising* 21, no. 4 (December 1992), 12.

6. Jane Pavitt, "In Goods We Trust," and "Branding the Individual," in *Brand .new*, ed. Jane Pavitt (Princeton, N.J.: Princeton University Press, 2000), 38, 156.

7. According to Michael Gross, *Genuine Authentic: The Real Life of Ralph Lauren* (New York: HarperCollins, 2003), 5, "In 2002, its thirty-fifth year, Polo Ralph Lauren was a four-headed Hydra. It is a wholesale clothing company selling eight lines of clothing for men, from the rare, tasteful, top-priced Purple Label suits, the better-priced, logo-splattered and ubiquitous Polo Sport brands; three more lines for women; a licensing company with thirty-two separate deals for everything wearable, from men's jeans to toddler togs at every possible price, as well as luggage, golf bags, other leather goods, ties, underwear, loungewear, swimwear, shoes, gloves, scarves, eyeglasses, jewelry, hosiery, fragrances and cosmetics, furniture, sheets, other bedding, towels, other bath products, silverware and other tabletop items, hardware, antiques, lighting accessories, rugs and carpets, and paint. There are even silver-clad $150,000 Lauren-customized Airstream trailers, and limited edition, numbered replicas of a 1909 teddy bear. Many assume that a line of food products (Lauren has seven hundred head of cattle on his Colorado ranch), and a collection of Ralph Lauren hotels will be the next products to carry one of his brands: Ralph Lauren, Polo, Polo Jeans Co., Polo Sport, Ralph Lauren Sport, Ralph, Lauren, Polo Golf, RLX, Double RL, and Chaps."

8. Michael Gross, *Genuine Authentic: The Real Life of Ralph Lauren*, 4.

9. Roland Marchand, *Advertising the American Dream: Making Way for Modernity, 1920–1940* (Berkeley: University of California Press, 1986), 165, 166.

10. Paul Fussel, *Class: A Guide Through The American Status System* (New York: Touchstone/Simon and Schuster, 1983), 71–73. Fussel writes: "As all salesmen recognize, if you're selling something it's better for your social class to be selling something archaic—like real wine or unpasteurized cheese or bread without preservatives or Renaissance art objects or rare books. Selling something old, indeed, almost redeems the class shame of selling anything at all." p. 73.

11. John Seabrook, *NoBrow: The Culture of Marketing. The Marketing of Culture* (London: Metheun, 2000), 50. Seabrook writes, that specifically, these images come ". . . from magazines, and books and movies about the British aristocracy, from Noel Coward plays, from the Cecil Beaton outfits in *My Fair Lady*, from Cary Grant in *The Philadelphia Story* and Grace Kelly in *High Society*, from *The New Yorker*."

12. Jim Collins, "No (Popular) Place Like Home?" in Jim Collins, *High-Pop: Making Culture into Popular Entertainment*, ed. (Malden, Mass.: Blackwell Publishers, 2002), 187.

13. Lynne Luciano, *Looking Good: Male Body Image in Modern America* (New York: Hill and Wang, 2001), 9.

14. Cited in John Seabrook, *NoBrow*, 51.

15. In *Landscapes of Power: From Detroit to Disney World* (Berkeley: University of California Press, 1993), 231, Sharon Zukin writes the following, very relevant passage, which resonates quite prominently in the Lauren universe:

> The stage-set landscape is a liminal space between nature and artifice, and market and place. It mediates between producer and consumer, a cultural object with real economic effect. The Disney landscape has in fact become a model for establishing both the economic value of cultural goods and the cultural value of consumer products. Just as the "World of Coca-Cola" museum at the corporate headquarters in Atlanta places an established consumer product in a narrative framework that renews its cultural legitimacy, so art museums have replaced their encyclopedic manner of display, which induces "museum fatigue," with story-telling strategies . . .

16. Witold Rybczynski, *Home: A Short History of an Idea* (New York: Viking/Penguin, 1986), 2, 3.

17. Gross, *Genuine Authentic*, 13.

18. Teri Agins, *The End of Fashion: The Mass Marketing of The Clothing Business* (New York: William Morrow and Company, 1999), 85.

19. Cited in Susan Caminiti, "Ralph Lauren: The Emperor Has Clothes," in *The Meaning of Dress*, eds. Mary Lynn Damhorst, Kimberly A. Miller, and Susan O. Michelman (New York: Fairchild Publications, 1999), 439.

20. Alison Lurie, *The Language of Clothes* (New York: Random House, 1981), 5.

21. William Leach, *Land of Desire: Merchants, Power, and the Rise of a New American Culture* (New York: Pantheon, 1993), 91.

22. Pamela Fiori, "Life is But a Dream," *Town & Country* (December 1996), 140.

23. Witold Rybczynski, *Home: A Short History of an Idea*, 11.

24. Fred Davis, *Fashion, Culture, and Identity* (Chicago: University of Chicago Press, 1992), 25.

25. Alison Lurie, *The Language of Clothes* (New York: Random House, 1981), 115–16.

26. Lurie, *The Language of Clothes*, 131–33.

27. Lurie, *The Language of Clothes*, 132, 133.

28. Jeffrey A. Tractenberg, *Ralph Lauren: The Man Behind the Mystique* (Boston/Toronto: Little Brown & Co., 1988), 91.

29. Michael Korda, *Horse People*, Cited in Barbara Kay, "Stop Subsidizing the Horsey Set," *The National Post* (Wednesday, August 18, 2004), A14.

30. Tractenberg, *Ralph Lauren*, 21.

31. Agins, *The End of Fashion*, 87.

32. Agins, *The End of Fashion*, 88.

33. Agins, *The End of Fashion*, 88.

34. James B. Twitchell, *Lead Us Into Temptation: The Triumph of American Materialism* (New York: Columbia University Press, 1999), 217.

35. Gross, *Genuine Authentic*, 257.

8

✛

Shopping As a Cultural Experience: Museums, Merchandising, and the Marking of Culture

Virtually every museum and gallery in existence has a gift shop where souvenirs, reproductions, knick-knacks, and other assorted merchandise are available for sale. Whether it is the Rijksmuseum in Amsterdam, The Metropolitan in New York, the Louvre in Paris, the Uffizi in Florence, or the Royal Ontario Museum in Toronto, an impressive selection of items is on sale to the public. Some of these offerings are tacky, yet most are blessed with a patina of class that is derived from the authority of art, culture, or archeological/historical capital. In other words, most of these objects "carry the imprimatur of good taste and historical significance that we associate with great museums."[1]

Of significance and concern to some is the fact that the museum was once thought of as a "commerce-free zone," a place above the impureness of money.[2] Given the fact that museum gift stores have become quite large and satellite shops dot the landscape, the conflation between going to the museum and going shopping is quite pronounced. One author boldly states, "Going to that museum is now more like visiting a shopping mall than a library, and hence a favorite tourist activity."[3] Gone are the somber galleries and dark lighting. Banished is the quiet and the contemplative environment. Now, it is often bright lights and interactive displays, flashy graphics, and all the trappings of mass-mediated culture.

In contradiction to this view, there has always been the suggestion that the museum had much in common with the Victorian department store.[4] Goods or objects behind glass and the ability to walk into a large cavernous space suggested common attributes. Since the invention of the department store, this separation of the retail environment and that of the museum has blurred. Their functions have been drawing together ever since. These two factors are the lines that must be straddled in today's social and cultural environment. Governing this is the fact that millions of dollars in revenue are generated for the maintenance of museums. According to one study, as much as twenty percent of derived income can be generated from these shops. Another source suggests that museum stores and gift shops have earned over two and a half times the revenue of admission and membership fees.[5] Museums have gotten into the retail trade in a big way. William Fox relates that there are now more than 1,800 museum stores in the United States alone.[6]

In some instances government subsidies have declined severely. In other cases the museum that has never received government funding now has to compete with other venues for the "attraction dollar." Virtually every renovation of a major museum comes complete with ample room for stores and shops, and numerous kiosks.[7] Beyond the commercial imperative, the rise of gift stores has often been guided by the elite orientation of museums. This is the attempt to disseminate the value of art and culture to the masses. For people to see the great works or to be informed by the display, a diffusion of cultural capital would be possible. By allowing a reproduction of a great work of art or an artifact of significance to be purchased, the appreciation of the original would only be increased.[8] A major contributing factor in the success of museum gift stores is simply that people want to bring home something unique or something beautiful that they may have seen inside the gallery or at least at the gift store.[9]

The Metropolitan Museum of Art in New York City has had a museum shop since 1871. It has grown to such a size that it is often compared to a small department store.[10] It now has a reputation as a commercial store that rivals other more traditional stores. People make special trips to this gift emporium as often as for the works of art within. Although certain critics have always feared this form of commercialism, the pull of money has been too strong. This major consideration is also linked to attendance. Museums have had to rethink their roles and many have come to the conclusion that because shopping is such a popular activity which is now so associated with entertainment, the expanded role of the museum store makes sense.[11] There are now MET stores situated throughout New York, nineteen in other states, and an online shop. The British Museum has an outlet at Heathrow Airport. The Louvre has 55 stores throughout France.[12] These off-premises stores account for significant income but also serve to accelerate the purchasing of simulations and reproductions of the museum's contents without the individual ever having to enter the museum itself.[13]

One barometer of how pervasive this process has become is to look at what the Vatican Museum at St. Peter's in Rome has allowed. There has been a full-fledged embracement of the consumption/shopping/entertainment ethos within the Holy See. All the treasures of the Vatican—religious documents, symbols, and icons—are now available to be purchased as reproductions. What was once the definitive display of Christian culture and 'beyond' the trappings of consumerism, is now, at least in one way, available to any visitor.[14]

Perhaps it was a natural progression in the scheme of consumer culture. Because shopping is such a popular activity, it seems almost natural to accommodate the average individual's consumption habits.[15] Merging the worlds of art and culture with the world of material culture can be deemed an inevitable process. The museum-in-the-mall concept starts to make sense if you want to attract people.[16] John Bentley Mays feels that there is absolutely nothing wrong with this process, in particular, because there is a "venerable history" behind it. Those who have perused the great palaces, museums, and cultural sites of Europe have always returned with symbols of what they have visited or what they have seen.[17]

One general assumption that affects this process is that the museum purchases of artistic or ancient provenance are often seen to be a classic middlebrow consumption habit. The same people who subscribe—or used to subscribe—to the Book of the Month Club and attend the odd Broadway show are those who purchase the reproductions.[18] It is this ability to bring home a piece of culture that often inspires the choice. People purchasing the tie with Van Gough's sun flowers, the coffee mug with Monet's water lilies or the reproduction of a 2,000-year-old Greek or Roman or Egyptian statue are able to bring home a touch of the culture contained within the museum. Every morning when they look at their Dianne Arbus agenda, they are reminded of the association with culture that that product gives them. According to one commentator, the reason for the expansion of the museum shops is simply that "people love this stuff." In line with the ethos of shopping as an entertainment experience, individuals get excited when they have the opportunity to make these purchases in these environments.[19] What sets the museum products apart in many cases is often their high quality and unique value. This reality or even this perception generates major revenues for museums. In turn it can be marketed as an exclusive luxury item not to be found anywhere else. According to Karen Von Hahn, 80 percent of the MET's products are exclusive designs, which are suggested by the curators of this venerable institution.[20]

Increasingly, the museum shop or gallery store has become a major focal point in the *raison d'etre* of the place. Museums are aware that many visitors bypass the actual galleries and make a beeline directly to the gift store in search of a souvenir, often the museum's best-known reproductions, without ever experiencing the actual contents of the museum proper.[21] The gift shop or museum store is now a very significant element of the cultural experience of museum going. No longer shunted aside or banished to some remote corner as an afterthought, this retail space now occupies a prominant position in the museum and art gallery environment.

Another factor in the rise of these stores is the fact that museums are places that one cannot touch the objects. Caressing a painting or sculpture is not acceptable. Glass enclosures bar people from the tactile longing to embrace. As such, the freedom to hold and to take home something that may remind someone of what was off limits may in fact be of great appeal.[22]

Since the 1940s these retail environments have grown in size, importance, and attractiveness. What the museum store sells is a popularized series of versions contained within the walls of the museum/gallery itself. As Neil Harris has observed, these stores often function as "commercial publicists" for the institution.[23] In some instances the museum store or the museum gift store has grown into an enormous operation, complete with catalogues, franchise outlets, and Web sites that generate substantial revenue.[24] There is even a whole subset of commercial culture dedicated to the merchandising of museum products. The Museum Store, found in numerous malls throughout North America, sells a variety of artistic and cultural offerings which range from a Mona Lisa stamp pad to a Venus De Milo paperweight. There is no end to the statuary and numerous collections from every culture on the globe.[25] One may feel that this kind of environment has a significant educational component to it. Simply walking through the shop, one is exposed to a watered-down version of Matthew Arnold's definition of culture.

Novelist Paul Rudnick, writes a wonderful passage about the allure of the museum gift store and the responses it can provoke:

> Gift shops were by far Joe's favorite part of any museum. At Christmas, Mrs. Reckler had always bought each of Joe's teachers a Museum of Modern Art date book. The Reckler home sported many museum exhibition posters, framed under glass. As a child, Joe had always collected postcards, hoarding his Monet *Waterlilies* and Unicorn tapestries the way others stockpiled their Mickey Mantles and Willie Mayses. Joe had always coveted the coffee-table books for sale at the larger museum shops. These ten-ton volumes, on Hockney's stage designs or the Treasures of the Prado, had always struck Joe as luscious. Shopping and museum going were closely related experiences. Both demanded curiosity and dedication and comfortable walking shoes. When Joe thought of his childhood, he thought of Lord & Taylor and *Guernica*. Mrs. Reckler introduced him to both.[26]

Rudnick's character, Joe Reckler, sees the world through the eyes of the consummate consumer, or perhaps more accurately, the definitive example of the purchaser of virtually everything. Whatever he sees is seen through the windows of stores. His relationship to art is intermingled with consumption. And he sees no problems with that correlation.

What are the consequences of merging art and commerce in the manner of a Rodin mug or a three musketeers chess set? On the one hand, the replica Aztec mask and the Picasso umbrella are one of the few ways people can 'bring home art' and live with culture everyday. Since virtually no one can afford the original, a reproduction is the next best thing.[27] The expense of coffee table books with their wonderful colorful plates has also become a factor in making these artistic knock-offs appealing. But, as Walter Benjamin observed, the uniqueness of the original is essentially watered down the more it is reproduced. Photographs and posters are one version, but the massive multiplication of imagery is another, especially in the form of coffee mugs, stationery, and pens.

The conflation of the roles of the museum and the gift store has its origins in the fact that by the end of the nineteenth century, and certainly in the twentieth century, the department store increasingly took on many of the characteristics of the museum, and the museum in many respects came to possess certain elements of the department store. This symbiotic relationship is still an ongoing phenomenon; for example, as John Seabrook has observed, the Pottery Barn takes on the characteristics of the museum in the way that "seeing in the physical world furniture you are already familiar with from its reproduced image in a catalog gives it a kind of aura it wouldn't ordinarily have."[28] Related to this there is also the eerie feeling that one experiences upon entering some museums. This is the 'unsure' phenomenon of being unaware if one is in fact in a store or possibly a gallery.[29] This is most frequently experienced when one enters certain fashion environments, with their sparse Zen-like offerings. In essence the fashion outlet or boutique is more like a private art gallery than a retail store. Niketown in Chicago, and the numerous Niketowns throughout North America, have become synonyms for the conflation of the museum and the retail outlet. As Donald Katz describes, the store has become a museum to Nike's version of sports culture: "Nike artifacts were displayed like objects in a state-of-the-art museum, with museum-style display copy underneath."[30]

Dietmar Steiner relates a story of how a visitor to the Guggenheim Museum's Soho branch, now a Prada store, had to walk through the famous and well-stocked museum store in order to get to the lobby to purchase tickets. The exhibit, of French post-war art began with small sculpture's which happened to be situated on pedestals. One of the sculptures, was taken off its pedestal and brought to the store's cash desk. The customer, or visitor, wanted to purchase the piece. He was informed of his faux pas. This story is telling of the fact that very often, the seamless boundaries between the store and the museum are in effect indistinguishable. "Museums," according to Steiner, "now sell as much as they show."[31]

One reason for the increased popularity and quantities of museums has as much to do with what they show as with anything. What this means is that the products of popular culture have become elevated to a level of acceptable status—fit for a museum. In the late eighties the explosion in the popularity of sports memorabilia initiated a level of unprecedented activity in the buying, selling, and acquisition of sports artifacts. The desire to own a jersey worn by a famous player, or to have a rare sports card, moved the focus from a few die-hard collectors into the mainstream. The focus on sports and sports celebrities by the mass media and the deification of numerous superstar athletes also accentuated this process. Thus, when Niketown began to display the shoes, clothes, medals, and other accessories of their celebrity/athlete endorsers in glass cases, with museum-like labels, the public was quite comfortable with what they were seeing, and in many cases came to the store solely to be a part of this mass culture museum store experience. Nike artifacts transitioned into art objects, complete with their glamourous aura.

The original Niketown in Chicago suggested to consumers that entering its doors would be an experience unlike anything else. The combination e-store, museum, and spectacle generated excitement and buzz, and for a while was the definitive "must-see" retail entertainment destination.[32] Beyond the glass display cases and the velvet ropes, there was much that Niketown had in common with the museum. "Employees," writes Lisa Penaloza, "were posted in each room like museum attendants." And, the "store was organized into a number of 'concept rooms' . . ."[33]

The Canadian Museum of Civilization is increasingly oriented around this consumption ethos. This institution has also gone in the direction of integrating entertainment models into its presentation of culture. According to Jill Delaney, there is now more than one type of gift store available in this Ottawa/Hull architectural landmark. There is the "typical museum shop" and also the "higher-end craft, artifact, and reproduction shop."[34] The same type of approach is utilized at the Art Gallery of Ontario, which has a massive gift shop devoted to everything from artifacts and reproductions to furniture and jewelry. The Royal Ontario Museum also has a number of different shops designated for different items, a major consideration for its newly renovated space. Delaney defends this approach at the Canadian Museum of Civilization by suggesting that, "these shops act as key tools in the dispersion of cultural knowledge and identity." The shops allow both Canadian and foreign visitors to take home an artifact (whether genuine or reproduction), which is a "totem symbolic of their initiation into Canadian culture."[35] Delaney's observation is a key reason why these shops are so popular, but it can also be applied as an excuse for the excessive commodification of culture.

This is a very significant point. By allowing an individual to purchase a reproduction, one is being acclimatized with culture. Does the act of purchasing an object d'art in a gift store become something crass, and the supposed opposite, purchasing a painting or print at an auction or in a private gallery become akin to going to the opera or ballet? Is the former a form of vulgar middlebrow indulgence, while the later is seen as culturally more appropriate? Who is one to judge where the line between the first ends and the line of the second begins? Is it the quality of the object or is it something more? If one is to factor in elitism, or snobbism, then it is something more. What this does do is erode the traditional distinctions of cultural capital set out so firmly by Bourdieu, which suggests that what is legitimate is highbrow and rich in cultural capital and what is not, ersatz or faux culture, is low in cultural capital.[36] An all-important point to this is that what people now define as culture are often the products of the mass media and goods that have been produced for some commercial reason. If "art is the stuff that generates shared experience,"[37] then what is being defined as artistic has to be commercial and has to be purchasable.

At the National Gallery of Canada a few years back, a major exhibit of French Impressionist paintings was almost designed around strategically placed gift shops. John Bentley Mays describe the scene and its consequences:

> There's a small one at the exit of the show—baited, like a leg-hold trap, with gorgeous cards, catalogues, posters. Then there's the main spectacle: the store near the museum entrance. What's amazing isn't the popping down of the luminous mauves and sensuous greens typical of Impressionist stylistics. After all, most of the souvenirs are beautifully and skillfully done. Rather, it's the sheer number and variety of things that are being Impressionized.[38]

This dimension of both quality and quantity changes somewhat the parameters of taste and acquisition. Mays contends that virtually every dominant art style, from Futurism to Abstract Expressionism has in some way or form moved from the walls and cases of museums and galleries onto the T-shirts, placemats, and of course, advertising formats. He feels that this is quite acceptable because it demonstrates that "a great art style is great because of the rich vocabulary of images it offers to people outside the citadel of High Art."[39] What occurs is that banal objects, utilitarian artifacts of everyday use, are significantly transformed and made much more aesthetically pleasing. This allows for the transmission of the ingredients of high art to transcend the confines of the museum. In turn, what occurs is that there is a seeping out of high art into the mainstream. The products available at the American chain store, Target, reinforce this.

Many consumers are now familiar with the aesthetic qualities of various artistic designers thanks to Target's employment of Todd Oldham, Phillipe Starck, and Michael Graves.[40] Starck, a cutting-edge designer known for his hotel and restaurant interiors, is quoted as saying, "My goal in this democratization of design is to make possible the most joyful and exciting things and experiences for the maximum number of people."[41]

This process has been delineated supremely by the Italian manufacturer of tableware, Alessi. In a very deliberate fashion, the company set out to create a high-culture manifestation of its image. This was done by employing designers such as Graves to create a link in the customers' minds of museum-like quality and refinement within their products.[42] Specific tea sets and other similar productions were initially destined for museums in their very unique and limited runs. They were in turn buttressed by books and catalogues that reinforced their association with cultural products for the discerning consumer. According to design historian Penny Sparke,

> the link with museum culture was a strategic way of blurring the boundaries between culture and commerce such that the goods which Alessi presented in specialist retail outlets resembled museum objects displayed solely for cultural purposes. The shops in which they chose to retail their goods often looked more like art galleries than shops.[43]

It was Andy Warhol, in his often-cited quip, who remarked that the differences between the department store and the museum were virtually nonexistent. Since he voiced this clever observation, things have not only converged more finely but have also taken on a life of their own. Perusing the books in any well-stocked bookstore, one can find a number of guides to off-beat museums and galleries. In essence, the acceptance of the museum ambience has grown considerably.

The museum may be said to have broken out of its elitist assumptions and was increasingly accessible to the mass public in the late 1970s with the rise and increasing frequency of the blockbuster exhibits such as the King Tutankhamen show. Museums are not just accessible to the cultural elite, but all over they have become venues for a wide array of corporate gatherings, product launches, and personal celebrations. As always ,though, the largest source of interest and revenue comes from their shops.[44] Needless to say, museums have grown in both quality and diversity of display.

According to one group of scholars, this increase in the variety and quantity of museums has much to do with the overlap of a number of factors. There is a large demand for the information that a museum provides and authenticates within its walls.[45] The legitimacy of having some artifact tucked into the confines of a museum gives it a reliable provenance. This is made popular by surrounding the information in "enjoyable and comprehensible experiential formats," which increase people's willingness to enter.[46]

Even the way objects are now displayed in both environments is quite similar. Special lighting focuses the gaze upon an object/product that is placed in a setting that could come from a museum display or that is in a store. The intention to bring these two together is deliberate. Looking in the window and gazing at the display are now virtually the same. Both carry a visual form of reverence. As James Twitchell has recognized:

> The luxury store window has now joined the museum wall in replacing the church fresco and reliquary as objects of the fervent gaze. People pausing by windows, doing what is dismissed as window shopping, bear an eerie similarity to spectators gazing in the museum . . .[47]

At the same time as the above has been going on, the influences of the store or retail model on the museum, the reverse or opposite is also true. Boutiques in department stores and small retail outlets that are often high end, are also utilizing the museum approach, showcasing a few things in an almost art-like atmosphere rather than as a bazaar. The porous lines that had previously been parts of two separate yet related spheres no longer have the same definitions. A definitive example of this is that stores now feature art exhibits that are promoted as such and that are not simply interior design. The upscale Toronto department store, Holt Renfrew has exhibited photographs from the Warhol Factory photo exhibit, and this is marketed as an art event.[48]

Museums now feature objects of consumer culture as often as "pure" art. This applied approach allows for corporations to fund the exhibit and the inevitable catalogue that accompanies the show, but also, has a tendency to draw large crowds. The San Francisco Museum of Modern Art's 2004/2005 show, "Glamour: Fashion, Industrial Design, Architecture," merged entertainment and consumer culture by exhibiting over one hundred objects, including the interior of a Prada store, a 2004 Bentley, a *Swarovski* chandelier, a Rolex watch and a number of evening gowns created by fashion designers.[49] The Guggenheim's recent showing of the "works" of Giorgio Armani was one of the most controversial in this new approach. The commercial influence was obvious, despite the impressive nature of the content.[50] The Musée des Beaux-arts in Montreal held a *Snoopy* exhibition that merged the art of the comic strip characters with "examples of spin-off products." As one commentator wrote at that time, it was "difficult to tell where the gallery ended and the shop began."[51]

For museums, one can convincingly argue that the move toward commercially viable activities, which may horrify members of the cultural elite but that bring in the crowds, are part of a survival strategy that is essential for their economic well-being. At the same time, the elitist, high culture assumptions about what art is and where it should be displayed now seem quaint and dated. Bringing culture to the masses, albeit in an entertainment format may be doing more to diffuse artistic intentions than would keeping it cloistered and segregated. The problem of defining the difference between art and merchandise, between marketing and culture, and between connoisseurship and consumption *will continue.*

NOTES

1. Lesley Haggin Geary and Grace Jidoun, "Museum Shops," *Money,* (December 2000), 186.

2. Carole Duncan, "Museums and Department Stores: Close Encounters," in *High-Pop: Making Culture into Popular Entertainment,* ed. Jim Collins (Malden, Mass.: Blackwell Publishers, 2002), 129.

3. Robyn Gillam, *Hall of Mirrors: Museums and the Canadian Public* (Banff, AB: The Banff Centre Press, 2001), xvii.

4. Jeanne Cannizzo, "Negotiated Realities: Towards an Ethnography of Museums," in *Living in a Material World: Canadian and American Approaches to Material Culture,* ed. Gerald Pocius (St. John's, Nfld.: Institute of Social and Economic Research, Memorial University of Newfoundland, 1991), 26.

5. Cited in Laura Byrne Paquet, *The Urge to Splurge: A Social History of Shopping* (Toronto: ECW Press, 2003), 202.

6. William L. Fox, *In the Desert of Desire: Las Vegas and the Culture of Spectacle* (Reno: University of Nevada Press, 2005), 36.

7. James B. Twitchell, *Branded Nation* (New York: Simon & Schuster, 2004), 198.

8. Ada Louise Huxtable, *The Unreal America: Architecture and Illusion* (New York: The New Press, 1997), 84.

9. Martin M. Pegler, *Lifestyle Stores* (New York: PBC/Rizzoli, 1996), 60.

10. George Ritzer, *Enchanting a Disenchanted World,* Second Edition (Thousand Oaks: Pine Forge, 2005), 22.

11. Sze Tsung Leong, ". . . And Then There Was Shopping," in *Harvard Design School Guide to Shopping, Project on the City 2,* directed by Rem Koolhaas (Koln: Taschen, 2001), 145. 146.

12. Cited in George Ritzer, *Enchanting a Disenchanted World,* 22.

13. Twitchell, *Branded Nation,* 250–51.

14. See Alexander Stille, *The Future of the Past* (New York: Farrar, Straus and Giroux, 2003).

15. See William L. Fox, *In the Desert of Desire,* 147.

16. Juliet Schor, *The Overworked American: The Unexpected Decline of Leisure* (New York: Basic Books, 1991), 108.

17. John Bentley Mays, "A Monet Umbrella for Just $19.95," *The Weekend Post,* (June 3, 2000), W6.

18. See Joan Shelly Rubin, *The Making of Middle/Brow Culture* (Chapel Hill: The University of North Carolina Press, 1992). On page 3, Shelly Rubin writes, ". . . Middle-class Americans in the mid-nineteenth century scrambled to purchase replicas of luxury items (carpets, upholstery, watches) in order to mimic the upper echelons of society. Such goods made it both easier to acquire an aura of refinement—to regard gentility itself as a commodity—and more difficult to sift imposters from the authentically respectable."

19. James B. Twitchell, *Lead Us into Temptation: The Triumph of American Materialism* (New York: Columbia University Press, 1999), 243.

20. Karen Von Hahn, "Museum Stores," *The Globe and Mail*, (November 1, 2003), L3.

21. See Leong, ". . . And Then There Was Shopping," 146, and Juliet Schor, *The Overworked American*, 48.

22. Laura Byrne Paquet, *The Urge To Splurge*, 203.

23. Neil Harris, *Cultural Excursions: Marketing Appetites and Cultural Tastes in Modern America* (Chicago: University of Chicago Press, 1990), 80.

24. Carole Duncan, "Museums and Department Stores: Close Encounters," 129.

25. Twitchell, *Lead Us into Temptation*, 238.

26. Paul Rudnick, *I'll Take It* (New York: Ballantine Books, 1989), 227.

27. Lucy R. Lippard, *On the Beaten Track: Tourism, Art and Place* (New York: The New Press, 1999), 92.

28. John Seabrook, *Nobrow: The Culture of Marketing, the Marketing of Culture* (London: Methuen, 2000), 172.

29. In her analysis of Niketown, Lisa Penaloza makes numerous references to this sense of confusion. See Lisa Penaloza, "Just Doing It: A Visual Ethnographic Study of Spectacular Consumption Behavior at Niketown," *Consumption, Markets and Culture*, Vol. 2, no. 4, 1999, 342.

30. Donald Katz, *Just Do It: The Nike Spirit in the Corporate World* (New York: Random House, 1994), 272.

31. Dietmar Steiner, "Promotional Architecture," *Architectural Design: Fashion and Architecture* 70, no. 6, (December 2000), 21.

32. Whether through word of mouth or publication information in magazines that deal with consumer arenas, this type of promotion is ongoing. A number of years ago, Dylan's Candy Store in New York, owned by Ralph Lauren's daughter, became the must-see retail site for Torontonians.

33. Lisa Penaloza, "Just Doing It: A Visual Ethnographic Study of Spectacular Consumption Behavior at Niketown," 377.

34. Jill Delaney, "Ritual Space in The Canadian Museum of Civilization: Consuming Canadian Identity," in *Lifestyle Shopping: The Subject of Consumption*, ed. Rob Shields (New York: Routledge, 1992), 136.

35. Jill Delaney, "Ritual Space in The Canadian Museum of Civilization: Consuming Canadian Identity," 136.

36. Juliet B. Schor, *The Overspent American: Upscaling, Downshifting, and the New Consumer* (New York: Basic Books, 1998), 29.

37. Twitchell, *Branded Nation*, 260.

38. John Bentley Mays, "A Monet Umbrella for Just $19.95," *The Weekend Post*, (June 3, 2000), W6.

39. Mays, "A Monet Umbrella for Just $19.95," W6.

40. See Michael J. Silverstein and Neil Fiske, *Trading Up: The New American Luxury* (New York: Portfolio/Penguin, 2003), 176, and Michelle Lee, *Fashion Victim: Our Love-Hate Relationship with Dressing, Shopping and the Cost of Style* (New York: Broadway Books, 2003), xix.

41. Cited in Laura Rowley, *On Target: How the World's Hottest Retailer Hit a Bull's-Eye* (New Jersey: John Wiley & Sons, 2003), 37.

42. Penny Sparke, *An Introduction to Design and Culture: 1900 to the Present*, Second Edition, (London: Routledge, 2004), 174.

43. Sparke, *An Introduction to Design and Culture*, 174.

44. John Naisbitt and Patricia Abundene, *Megatrends 2000* (New York: William Morrow, 1990), 69, 80–82.

45. One should not lose sight of the fact that many of the most famous museum collections have been composed by "taking" artifacts from others who could not defend or assert their rights. See Mark Moss, "Indiana Jones and the Museums of Imperialism," *Popular Culture Review* 12, no. 2 (August 2001).

46. John H. Falk and Lynn D. Dierking, *Learning from Museums: Visitor Experiences and the Making of Meaning* (Walnut Creek, Calif.: Altamira Press/Rowman & Littlefield Publishers, Inc., 2000), 2.

47. Twitchell, *Branded Nation*, 231.

48. Tralee Pearce, "Hospitality Retail," *The Globe and Mail*, (September 18, 2004), L1.

49. "The Gilded Age," *The New York Times Style Magazine*, Design (Fall 2004), 126.

50. Twitchell, *Branded Nation*, 241.

51. Robyn Gillam, *Hall of Mirrors: Museums and the Canadian Public*, 220.

Conclusion

S ince the 1980s, with regular bursts of the bubble, the acceptability of the enjoyment of shopping and the celebration of accumulation of goods, especially high-status purchases, has increased. The glorification of wealth, and not just in the West, has much to do with this trend. *The Robb Report*, a high-end showcase for the most exclusive and expensive items, from cars to watches to homes, dovetails with television shows that profile stores, shopping, and material culture. What this may be is a reversal or perhaps a perversion of Weber's Protestant Ethic thesis. According to Colin Campbell, what the Protestant Ethic thesis suggested was not a prohibition on the acquisition of things and the "accumulation of wealth," but the no-no was the enjoyment of possessions.[1] Society has moved away from the guilt and the contriteness associated with shopping and purchasing. A form of vague hedonism pervades our universe and is expressed through shopping as an entertainment experience.

A significant amount of shopping still involves the most prosaic activities, what Daniel Miller calls provisioning.[2] This is the humdrum, last - minute purchase of the staple, the one somebody must make at an inconvenient time, in essence the outing antithetical to leisure and entertainment. But increasingly, shopping has become accepted as a viable entertainment/leisure activity. James Rouse, one of the more innovative mall developers, recognized this a number of years ago and summed up this change by stating, "shopping is increasingly entertainment and a competitor with other entertainment choices. In a circumstance of delight, it gratifies a need that might otherwise be met by a trip to New York, or a weekend at the beach."[3] In his important and original study of *fin-de-siecle* public amusements and their correlation to public sociability, David Nasaw concludes his study by suggesting on the one hand that "We no longer 'go out' as much as we once did." We have all of our amusements in our homes, from computers to compact discs, which enhance our domestic environment. Yet Nasaw makes a key point, extraordinarily relevant for the themes of this work. He opines the following:

> The public amusement centers that survive and prosper are those that have been reconceived, repackaged and transported out of town. The symbol of public sociability in the late twentieth century is not the picture palace or amusement park, but the enclosed shopping mall.[4]

Going to the mall to browse for a few hours is more than just 'killing time.' This idea highlights, again, the difference between the mundane 'doing the shopping' and the more involved 'going shopping.' As Jane Pavitt has written, "going shopping might be an adventure, doing shopping a chore; we attach much more significance to the purchases we make when we are shopping for leisure; these are the goods that may give us identity or bring us to a sense of belonging."[5] For some men, shopping has replaced hunting in the traditional sense, while for women, shopping has become a form of gathering. Looking for *the bargain* has become equated with bagging the boar. The thrill of the hunt has now been transferred to the world of consumption.[6]

What is important to recognize regarding shopping, and in particular, shopping at the mall, is the fact that people wish to enter into 'fantasy' worlds that take them beyond their ordinary everyday encounters. Seeing a film that moves one into this realm is a very gratifying sensation. As an entertainment experience, shopping can allow the individual to move in an environment that is beyond the threshold of the ordinary.[7] Arcades and other entertainment attractions found in stores and in malls are no longer simply places for the kids. They are there to "babysit" men who often do not wish to be there but are nonetheless there on a regular basis.[8] What is created in the fusion of entertainment and retail is a safe yet exciting environment of a new atmosphere, where consumption is accompanied by entertainment in often-magical terms.[9] The increased establishment of major arcade-like structures in malls and other retail venues is indicative of the changes taking place. Miniature theme parks and other virtual environments have become staples in new malls, along with theaters and themed restaurants. The fact that huge walking clubs are increasingly part of the mall landscape, not to mention concierge services and other perks, means that more and more people will come.[10] They not only appeal to certain non-shoppers but rather become supplements to the shopping as an entertainment experience.[11]

Over ten years ago, one retail analyst suggested that entertainment is something that has been completely incorporated into every facet of "our" experience. In the North American context, and increasingly around the globe, some aspect of entertainment permeates our consciousness almost twenty-four hours a day. Presciently, he remarked, "People have come to expect to be entertained. In the minds of American consumers, the pursuit of happiness had developed into the right of entertainment."[12]

As society searches for more entertainment experiences, the impact on shopping will increase. Novelty and newness, diversion and amusement will become fully intertwined with shopping in order to create the most effective environments and to instill a level of comfort and attraction that is quite pronounced. If one looks at the evolution from the department store to the mall to the e-store, this process is well on its way.

It is increasingly being thought that the new way to appeal to shoppers is to lure them in with all the entertainment trappings that are conceivable. This move, to transform all of shopping "into an entertainment event, an escape from everyday life," seems quite promising to those involved with the activities surrounding shopping. If people are willing to pay to go to Dave & Buster's or to throw money around at the Rainforest Café or the Harley Davidson Café's merchandise, the enhancement of the "entertainment component" of many retail environments will only continue.[13] The creation of environments, such as in Las Vegas, that are fully designed as a shopper's escape where the pleasures and fantasies of unabashed consumption have been created is possibly just the first step.

As developers and designers think of new ways to make shopping an entertainment experience the boundaries between old, established parameters will disappear. City spaces will blend into atmospheres which promote shopping in subtle and sophisticated ways. Urban renewal will become enmeshed with creating more novel shopping experiences, further blurring the lines between consumption, entertainment, and leisure. To some extent, post-modern metropolises such as Shanghai have already become the full-fledged extension of this process. The city, in these instances is a shopping Mecca of unparalleled entertainment experience. One can bargain in the famous markets and be entertained or one can peruse a wide array of shopping experiences that are predicated on the city itself as the ultimate shopping mall. These zones become famous for their bargains, their sophistication or their extravagance. And they have come to rival cultural, artistic, and heritage sites in their appeal. Just as important in seeing the colonial buildings on the Bund in Shanghai, one must walk down the pedestrian mall on Nanjing road. It has become commonplace to say that if you did not see Nanjing, you did not see Shanghai. But even a visit to some ruin or site in the countryside now includes shopping. Whether a trinket from a souvenir stand, or a work of art from a sculptor, no longer can travel be oriented around just seeing. One *must and does*, shop.

It is not just the mainstream of urban culture that has given way to this shopping-as-an-entertainment focus. Small towns that wish to attract the tourist, or the weekend shopper, spend a lot of money and time on projects that attract potential shoppers. These miniature "main streets" have been polished up and converted to appeal to the perception of certain shoppers and their expectations about what a small town is all about. The antique stores, craft shops, and cafes that now line many a main street in and around small towns provide the comfort and convenience of urban entertainment shopping. As has been mentioned, along with the worlds of Ralph Lauren, this is a process that critics of marketing have termed "restroscaping."[14] The use of nostalgia and history to evoke a positive feeling makes shopping a pleasing entertainment experience.

One of the indications that shopping is a supremely popular entertainment experience has always been the grand opening of retail establishments. Whenever a new mall or new store is launched, it becomes an 'event.' The opening of a new boutique on Madison Avenue, designed by a superstar decorator, precipitates a huge gathering. The opening of some electronic superstore becomes something 'to do.' This process has a long, continuous history. Shopping environments are key centerpieces in many communities; thus, when a new store opens, it is an 'event.' When Filene's opened its Boston store in 1912, almost a quarter of a million people showed up.[15] The opening of the Swedish department store H&M in Toronto in the fall of 2004 was not nearly as crowded, but thousands did show up. The megamall, Vaughan Mills, north of Toronto, was profiled by numerous television stations and featured in all the dailies. In interviews with people, many mentioned that they were either planning a trip "up there" or actually going to go in a coming weekend. According to the *Toronto Star*, 80, 000 people showed up on the first day, and as many as 300,000 came to the mall in its first three days of operation.[16] Whenever a new store—especially a large and sophisticated one—opens, the press covers the opening and interviews celebrities and the public at large. Like the film openings, these events have become significant preludes to what is inside. People want to know and want to see and explore. Shopping has become part of the entertainment experience.

The not-so-simple appeal of going to look at windows of certain retail establishments still exerts a pull in many urban areas. In the 1990s in New York, Simon Doonan's windows for upscale retailer Barneys drew thousands to the store on 17th Street during the Christmas season. Tourists and New Yorkers made the trek to the store just to see what everyone was talking about. One could indeed make the argument that fashion, art, and retail had blended into a supremely potent version of shopping as entertainment experience.[17]

One of the concerns that those in the retail industry voiced as a consequence of the full-blown merging of shopping with entertainment is that in some cases the levels to which retailers are willing to go and shoppers have come to expect are eroding the essence of retailing. As one industry insider has stated, "After all, entertainment for its own sake has no value. As retailers, we must continually ask ourselves: Are we losing sight of the products we're selling? Are we forgetting the 'merchandise' in 'merchandising?'"[18] Concerns such as these may be extended in the coming years, but as virtually every facet of mass and high culture merges into some form of shopping experience—as shopping itself becomes the definitive entertainment endeavor—the boundaries will continue to blur.

Films, art, amusement rides, simulated attractions, and video games will become vehicles for shopping in ways that have not been contemplated. The synergies between new media and mass culture will accelerate to produce a variety of shopping experiences that will make going to the mall even closer than going to Disney World. What Niketown and other e-retailers have done to enhance this process will only expand continuously, bounded only by the designer's imagination and the shoppers' continued willingness to be enthralled.

Shopping channels and Web sites offer a plethora of items that can be ordered and shipped in twenty-four hours. Like the museums with their gift stores, even highbrow public broadcasting has followed suit. PBS has its own on-line store, with videos, books, and tote bags. It is just a matter of time before "living in television," as far as a consumer, becomes real. One can foresee a time when watching a TV show, if one likes what the particular character is wearing, one could simply access the information about the jeans or the shirt and order it without moving off the couch. If one sees a book in the corner of the TV screen picture, perhaps that also could be purchased. Perhaps an indication that this is already happening is suggested by the British Home Shopping TV network, which ran the slogan, "The department store you come home to."[19]

It is possible to buy merchandise at virtually every conceivable entertainment venue. At the ballpark or hockey stadium, at a rock concert, in a gallery, at a university, there is always a place to pick up a sweatshirt or a jacket. The post office sells commemorative coins and stamps, bars and restaurants all have merchandise for sale, of one kind or another. Virtually every cultural zone, occasion, or outing of any viable creation has something for sale. At charitable gatherings and even commemorative events, there is something to buy, something to look at, and something to shop for. World Wildlife Fund donations now come with a hip T-shirt; contributing to Lance Armstrong's cancer rehabilitation charity means you get a very cool yellow rubber bracelet. [Shopping in many different forms has become an entertainment experience.]

The process of buying as a component of leisure will only increase. As the quote by Sze Tsung Leong, "shopping has methodically encroached on a widening spectrum of territories so that it is now, arguably, the defining activity of public life,"[20] found at the opening of this work implies that shopping is an integral part of not just the entertainment component of life, but also of most every facet.

NOTES

1. Colin Campbell, *The Romantic Ethic and the Spirit of Modern Consumption* (Oxford: Basil Blackwell, 1987), 102.

2. See Daniel Miller, *A Theory of Shopping* (Ithaca, N.Y.: Cornell University Press, 1998).

3. Cited in Ira G. Zepp Jr., *The New Religious Image of Urban America: The Shopping Mall as Ceremonial Center,* Second Edition (Niwot: University Press of Colorado, 1997), 98.

4. David Nasaw, *Going Out: The Rise and Fall of Public Amusements* (Cambridge, Mass.: Harvard University Press, 2002), 255.

5. Jane Pavitt, "Branding the Individual," in *Brand.new*, ed. Jane Pavitt (Princeton, N.J.: Princeton University Press, 2000), 156.

6. Candace Fertile, "The Oldest Profession: Shopping," in *Pop Can: Popular Culture in Canada*, eds. Lynne Van Luven and Priscilla L. Walton (Scarborough, ON: Prentice Hall, 1999), 81.

7. Robert R. Wilson, "Playing and Being Played: Experiencing West Edmonton Mall," in *Pop Can: Popular Culture in Canada*, eds. Lynne Van Luven and Priscilla L. Walton (Scarborough, ON: Prentice Hall, 1999), 85.

8. Thomas Hine, *I Want That! How We All Became Shoppers* (New York: HarperCollins, 2002), 27.

9. Iain Borden, "Fashioning the City: Architectural Tactics and Identity Statements," *Architectural Design: Fashion and Architecture* 70, no. 6 (December 2000): 14.

10. Philip Langdon, "The Evolution of Shopping," *The American Enterprise* 11, no. 2 (March 2000): 36.

11. See Stephen Kline, Nick Dyer-Witheford, and Greig De Peuter, *Digital Play: The Interaction of Technology, Culture, and Marketing,* (Montreal: McGill-Queen's University Press, 2003), 232.

12. Eugene Christiansen, cited in Donald Shillingburg, "Entertainment Drives Retail," *Architectural Record* (August 1994), 82.

13. Thomas Hine, *I Want That!* 200.

14. Stephen Brown, "No Then There: Of Time, Space and the Market," in *Time, Space, and the Market: Retroscapes Rising*, eds. Stephen Brown and John F. Sherry Jr. (Armonk, Conn.: M.E. Sharpe, 2003), 3.

15. Ann Satterthwaite, *Going Shopping: Consumer Choices and Community Consequences*, (New Haven: Yale University Press, 2001), 45.

16. See "Shopping," *The Toronto Star* (Sunday, December 26, 2004).

17. Simon Doonan, *Confessions of a Window Dresser* (New York: Viking/Callaway, 1998), 122.

18. Jody Patraka, "Foreword," to *Lifestyle Stores*, Martin M. Pegler, (New York: PBC/Rizzoli, 1996).

19. David Morley, "Theories of Consumption in Media Studies," in *Acknowledging Consumption*, ed. Daniel Miller, (London: Routledge, 1986), 316.

20. Sze Tsung Leong, ". . . And Then There Was Shopping," in *Harvard Design School Guide to Shopping, Project on the City 2*, directed by Rem Koolhaas, (New York: Taschen, 2001), 129.

Index

About the Author

Mark Moss is chair of the General Arts and Science Program at Seneca College in Toronto, Canada. He holds a master's degree in environmental studies from York University and a doctorate in history of education from Ontario Institute for Studies in Education of the University of Toronto. Dr. Moss is the author of *Manliness and Militarism*. He has published essays on culture, society, and the history of ideas and teaches courses in a wide variety of disciplines. His current research interests deal with visual history as well as an examination of contemporary masculinity. Prior to entering the academic realm, he worked for a diverse array of retail concerns and it is there that he began to critically examine the appeal of shopping.